SEASONED
With Soul

Table Of Contents

COCKTAILS

Pineapple Seduction 1
Passion Twist Margaritas 2
Royal Rose Mimosa 3
House Special Sangria 4
Kool Cups for Grown Ups 5

APPETIZERS

Spicy Alfredo Chicken Wings 6
Honey Jerk Wings 7
Peach Crown Royal Wings 9
Bang Bang Chicken Tenders 11
Lemon Pepper Wet Wings 13

QUICK BITES

Cajun Seafood Egg Rolls 15
Smoked Cajun Crab Dip 17
Buffalo Lemon Pepper Salmon Tenders 18
Blackened Salmon Deviled Eggs 20
Cajun Caesar Salad Boats 22
Fried Green Tomatoes with Bacon Jam Dip 24
Garlic Parmesan Lobster Tails 26
Jalapeno Lime Corn on the Cob 28
Boudin Stuffed Biscuits 29

SANDWICHES & BURGERS

Surf and Turf Burger 31
Seafood Melt 33
Blackened Cod Sandwich 35
Hot Honey Salmon Club 36
The LOX Melt 40

BRUNCH FAVORITES

Loaded Southern Seafood Grits 42
Jerk Chicken & Sweet Potato Cornbread Waffles 44
Brunchaholic 46
Seafood Fried Rice 48
Smothered Catfish Shrimp Dinner 49

PASTA

Rasta Pasta	51
Creamy Seafood Lasagna	53
Italian Sausage Stuffed Shells	55

SAVORY & SUPPLE

Garlic & Herb Turkey Wings	57
Red Wine Braised Short Ribs	59
Sweet & Zesty Baked Chicken	61
Parmesan Crusted Tuscan Chicken	63
Loaded Seafood Baked Potatoes	65
Tequila Lime Chicken	67
Honey Lime Jalapeno Chicken	69

SIDES

Sticky-Icky Bourbon Candied Yams	71
Soulful & Southern Collard Greens	72
Gourmet Lobster Mac and Cheese	73
Cheesy Au Gratin Potatoes	75

HOLIDAY MUST-HAVES & DESSERTS

Honey Baked Ham	77
Seafood Cornbread Dressing	79
Air Fried Cornish Hens Two Ways	81
Henny-Nog	83
Cajun Fried Turkey	85
Sweet Potato Cheesecake	87
Bad & Boozy Banana Pudding	89
Red Velvet Pound Cake	91
Peach Crown Cobbler Rolls	93
Maple Bacon Glazed Donuts	95
Bacon PB&J French Toast	97

Pineapple Seduction

This recipe is a refreshing and fantastic cocktail that is simple enough for any given day. It takes seconds literally to prepare, and it tastes so damn good!
It's tropically sweet and perfect for the summer get together!
The flavor combination of the vanilla Bumbu Rum, fruity Malibu Rum, and sweet pineapple is addicting sure will have you coming back for more!

Serving: 2 drinks
Equipment: shaker, 2 glasses
Total time: 5 minutes

Ingredients

- 1/3 cup ice cubes
- 1 shot Bumbu Rum
- 1 shot Malibu Rum
- 2 Tbsp Pineapple Syrup*
- 1 cup fresh pineapple juice
- Garnish: Tajin seasoning*, 2 pineapple slices, 2 lime slices

Direction

- Rim the glasses with Tajin seasoning and set them aside.
- Add ice cubes, rum, pineapple syrup, and fresh pineapple juice to a shaker. Shake well.
- Strain it into Tajin-rimmed glasses.
- Garnish with pineapple and lime slices.

Note:
Pineapple Syrup*: you can replace it with 1/4 cup of extra pineapple juice & 2 tsp of white sugar
Tajin seasoning: if you don't have it, use rim salt and dried red chili pepper powder.

Passion Twist Margaritas

Let's turn this thing up a few notches with the crowd pleaser Passion Twist Margaritas. The strawberry flavor mix effortlessly with the Casamigos Resposado!

Serving:
2 large

Equipment:
blender, 2 large margarita glasses

Total time:
5 minutes

Ingredients

- 1 cup ice-cubes (add more if you like a thicker margarita)
- 2 shots Casamigos Resposado tequila
- 1 shot Gloria Margarita Mix
- 1/2 cup Margarita Mix, Strawberry flavor (more mix will cut the alcohol taste)
- Garnish: rim salt, 2-4 lime slices

Direction

- Rim the margarita glasses with salt and set aside.
- Add ice, tequila, and margarita mixes to a blender.
- Blend well.
- Strain it into salt-rimmed glasses and garnish with lime slices.
- Let's let the party started!

Royal Rose Mimosa

OK SO BOOM CHECK THIS OUT! I'll start by saying "Drink Responsibly" this drink is not for the weak and frail. Classic mimosa with a twist! It's perfect for rose and mimosa lovers! You just need two minutes……. let's stay focused y'all….. I mean just two minutes to make this drink that everyone will love for sure!
Follow these simple steps to amplify your "Sunday Funday" brunch festivities!
Serving: 4-6
Equipment: shaker, 4-6 serving glasses
Total time: 2 minutes

Ingredients

- 1/4 cup Royal Crown Peach
- 1/4 cup Grand Marnier liqueur
- 1/4 cup Hennessy V.S.O.P
- 1/2 cup orange juice
- 4 Tbsp honey
- 1 bottle Luc Belaire Luxe Sparkling Rose

Direction

- • In a shaker, add Royal Crown, Grand Marnier liqueur, Hennessy, orange juice, and honey. Shake well.
- Gently pour about 60% in each glass of Rose, then fill in the rest with the liquor mixture from the shaker. Cheers!

House Special Sangria

Cord is in a kitchen House Special and NO shaker is needed!
This sangria is loaded with the goods for sure! Make it for a special date night, brunch, pool party, or "Netflix & Chill" …
Serving: 1 large glass
Total time: 2 minutes

Ingredients

- 1/2 cup ice cubes
- 1 shot Hennessy Cognac Privilege VSOP
- 1/2 cup Madria Sangria
- 1/2 cup Stella Rose

Gashing: handful berries (strawberries, blueberries, blackberries)

Direction

- Add ice cubes to a serving glass.
- Pour Hennessy, followed by Sangria and Rose. Gently mix with a fork or spoon, and enjoy.

Optional: garnish the rim with berries!

Kool Cups for Grown Ups

This drink is sure to transport you immediately to childhood nostalgia (minus the Hennessy.) It's sweet, refreshing, and boozy! I'll have two please!

Serving: 8-10

Equipment:
shaker, large pitcher, blender

Prep time: 10 minutes

Chill time: 8-12 hours

Ingredients

- 1 packet Kool-Aid Watermelon
- 1 packet Kool-Aid Cherry
- Sugar to taste
- Juice from one lemon
- 2 cups fresh strawberries
- 1 shot for one cup Vanilla Crown Royal Whiskey
- 1 shot for one cup Hennessy

Direction

- Prepare the Kool-Aid packets according to the direction with water, and pour them into a large pitcher. Add sugar and juice from one lemon.
- In a blender, blend fresh strawberries. Then spoon them on the bottom of each serving cup, about 3 Tbsp to each cup.
- In a shaker, blend Crown Royal and Hennessy Whiskey (one shot each) with about 1 cup of Kool-Aid.
- Gently pour this blend over the strawberries in serving cups.
- Repeat with remaining Kool-Aid and alcohol.
- Place these Kool Cups for Grown-Ups into a freezer for 6-12 hours before serving.

Spicy Alfredo Chicken Wings

This recipe combines everything you love about a traditional homemade Alfredo sauce, but with a Cajun twist!

Serving: 2

Equipment:
Large deep pan/skillet, medium pot

Prep time: 10 minutes

Cook time: 20 minutes

Total time: 30 minutes

Ingredients

- 1.5 pounds chicken wings
- 1 Tbsp All-Purpose Grill Mates*
- 1 tsp smoked paprika
- 1 Tbsp McCormick Salt-Free Garlic & Herbs Seasoning
- 1 cup cooking oil

For the sauce:
- 2 Tbsp butter
- 1/2 cup heavy cream
- 2 tsp All Purpose Grill Mates*
- 1 tsp garlic powder
- Handful Parmesan cheese
- Pinch cayenne pepper

Direction

- • Season the wings with Grill Mates, smoked paprika, and McCormick Seasoning.
- Preheat the skillet with oil over medium to medium-high heat, then add wings.
- Fry them for 8-10 minutes on each side.
- Remove the wings from the pan, set aside.

For the sauce:
- Preheat a pot with butter and add Grill Mates, paprika, and garlic powder.
- Reduce the heat to a low and simmer the sauce for 2 minutes.
- Add Parmesan cheese and a pinch of cayenne pepper. Stir and remove from the heat.

To assemble:
- Remove the wings from the oil, then allow them to drain on a paper towel or wire rack.
- Toss the wing with sauce and serve!

Note:
All-Purpose Grill Mates: you can replace it with ¼ tsp of each: salt, onion, and garlic powder.

Honey Jerk Wings

If you've been rocking with me since the beginning, then you know I love honey! Here's what happens when you mix two of my favorite flavors together on a chicken wing! Pure honey & jerk spices combine to create a finger licking good taste! Yesss Lawd!

Serving:
4 servings (5 wings each)

Equipment:
large deep pan/skillet, medium pot

Prep time: 5 minutes
Cook time: 15 minutes
Total time: 20 minutes

Ingredients

- 2 pounds chicken wings
- 1 Tbsp All-Purpose Grill Mates*
- 1 tsp smoked paprika
- 1/2 tsp regular paprika
- 2 tsp Walkerswood Traditional Jamaican Jerk sauce mild
- 1 Tbsp McCormick Salt-Free Garlic & Herbs Seasoning*
- 1-2 cups cooking oil

For the sauce:

- 1 tsp Frank's Red Hot (Honey Garlic sauce)
- 1/3 cup honey

To serve:
- Ranch dressing to taste & celery sticks

Direction

- Season the wings with Grill Mates, smoked paprika, regular paprika, Walkerswood, and McCormick Seasoning. (To optimize flavor, marinate wings for at least 1 hour.) **This is optional**
- Preheat the skillet with oil over medium heat, then add wings.
- Fry them for 8-10 minutes on each side.
- Remove the wings from the pan, set aside to drain on a paper towel or wire rack.

For the sauce:
- In a large bowl, whisk honey garlic sauce and honey.

To serve:
- Once wings are ready, add them to the bowl with sauce and stir well.
- Serve immediately with Ranch dressing to taste & celery sticks.

Note:

All-Purpose Grill Mates: you can replace it with ¼ tsp of each: salt, onion, and garlic powder.

McCormick Salt Free Garlic & Herbs Seasoning: if you don't have it, use an equal amount of each (pinch): oregano, parsley, rosemary, dried basil, red pepper flakes, onion powder, and smoked paprika.

Peach Crown Royal Wings

Make your game nights (or any occasion) great with these Peach Crown Royal Wings! Each crispy chicken wing is coated in garlicky, smoky seasonings that are mouthwatering! They are fried to perfection and then tossed in a spicy-sweet sauce! You will be "sipping" whiskey with every bite of these wings…. Bussin!
Serving: 4-6

Equipment
Large bowl, large skillet, tongs
Prep time: 5 minutes
Cook time: 20 minutes
Total time: 25 minutes

Ingredients

For the wings:
- 1.5-2 pounds chicken wings, washed
- 1 pack Goya Sazon seasoning
- 2 tsp smoked paprika
- 1 Tbsp garlic powder
- 1 Tbsp onion powder
- 2 cups cooking oil

For the sauce:
- 2 Tbsp Gochujang Sauce
- ¼ cup Peach Crown whisky
- 2 Tbsp soy sauce
- 1/4 cup honey
- 1/2 tsp chili powder
- ¼ cup brown sugar
- 1 Tbsp Worcestershire sauce

To assemble:
- 1/3 cup favorite Ranch or Blue cheese dressing

Direction

For the wings:
- In a large bowl, place chicken wings and season them with Goya, smoked paprika, garlic, and onion powder. Mix well to incorporate all flavors.
- Preheat large skillet with oil. Then carefully add wings to the hot oil using the tongs.
- Don't overcrowd the skillet as it will reduce cooking oil temperature, and the wings will end up being greasy and soggy.
- Fry the wings on medium-hot heat for 8-10 minutes on each side.
- Remove the chicken from the pan and let the wings rest on a paper towel or wire rack.
- Repeat with the remaining wings.

For the sauce:
- In a medium bowl, whisk all ingredients for the sauce. Set aside.

To assemble:
- Once chicken wings are done toss them with a sauce and serve immediately with Ranch or Blue cheese dressing.

Bang Bang Chicken Tenders

Fried chicken breast tossed in a delicious Truffle Mayo based sauce with added flavors of sweet chili, honey, hot sauce and garlic! Letssss Gooo!

Serving: 4

Equipment:
Baking cooking tray, 2 large bowls, large spoon or spatula, large skillet, tongs, paper towel, sauce pan, 4 serving plates

Prep time: 30 minutes
Cook time: 25 minutes
Total time: 55 minutes

Ingredients

For the chicken tenders:
- 1 cup cooking oil
- 4 chicken breasts, skinless, boneless
- 1 ½ Tsp Belay & Bell Nashville Hot seasoning
- 1 tsp Old Bay Seasoning Garlic & Herbs
- 1 tsp Louisiana Hot Sauce, original
- 1 tsp garlic powder
- 4 eggs, beaten

For the dry batter:
- 1 cup corn starch
- 1 cup white flour
- 1 Tbsp Old Bay Seasoning Garlic & Herbs
- 2 tsp hot sauce
- 1 tsp garlic powder
- 1 tsp onion powder

For the sauce:
- 1 stick of butter
- 1/3 cup sweet chili sauce
- 2 Tbsp "Truff" Black Truffle infused mayonnaise
- 1 Tbsp "Truff" hot sauce

- 1 Tbsp honey
- 2 garlic cloves, minced

Direction

For the chicken tenders:
- Slice the chicken breast into large thick long strips.
- Place them in a large bowl, adding all seasoning and beaten eggs.
- Mix well, using your hands or spatula. Set aside. For the dry batter:
- In a large bowl, mix flour with corn starch. Incorporate Old Bay, hot sauce, garlic, and onion powder.

For the sauce:
- Preheat a saucepan with butter. Add sweet chili sauce and hot sauce. Mix well and add the rest of the ingredients to the sauce.

Assemble:
- Take a chicken tender, dip into a dry batter.
- Shake any excess flour.
- Preheat a large chicken with cooking oil.
- Using tongs, carefully place chicken on a pan and fry on medium heat for 5 minutes on each side.
- Lay chicken on a paper towel to drain any excess fat. Repeat with remaining chicken.
- Place cooked chicken in a large bowl and pour the sauce over them. Toss to combine.
- Enjoy!!

Note:
Minced garlic: you can mince 2 large garlic cloves or use 1 Tbsp Spice Worlds Minced Garlic Squeeze brand.

Lemon Pepper Wet Wings

Top 2 lemon pepper wings that you'll come across… But this is NOT number 2! Let's get straight to it.

Serving: 4

Equipment: large bowl, air fryer, medium pot

Prep time: 5 minutes
Cook time: 25 minutes
Total time: 30minutes

Ingredients

For the chicken:

- 2 lb. chicken wings (cut into drumbeats and flats)
- ½ cup potato starch
- 3 Tbsp baking powder
- 2 sticks of butter
- 2 Tbsp Cajun Seasoning, unsalted
- 1 Tbsp smoked paprika
- 1 Tbsp. Old Bay
- 2 Tbsp. garlic powder
- 1-2 Tbsp onion powder
- 1 small lemon for zest & juice

For the sauce:
- 2 sticks of butter
- Drizzle of Frank's Red Hot sauce
- 1 Tbsp smoked paprika
- 2 tsp minced garlic1 tbsp. Old Bay
- 2 Tbsp. garlic powder
- 1-2 Tbsp onion powder
- Pinch fresh parsley

Direction

For the chicken:
- In a large bowl, combine all ingredients except for parsley and butter.
- Mix ingredients until each piece of chicken is evenly coated.
- Assemble chicken pieces into your air fryer in one single layer.
- Cook it at 400 degrees for 20-25 minutes, flipping halfway through.

For the sauce:
- While the chicken is cooking, place 2 sticks of butter and all spices for lemon pepper sauce into a pot.
- Melt it on medium heat.
- Once the butter has melted, reduce heat to low, and stir every 5 minutes until wings are done.

To serve:
- Toss wings and sauce in a bowl until they are evenly coated.
- Plate food and enjoy!

Cajun Seafood Egg Rolls

ALRIGHT SO BOOM LETS GET IT! Your guest will LOVE these Cajun Seafood Egg Rolls, I can guarantee they'll be gone in a MISSISSIPPI SECOND! Crispy egg rolls fried to perfection, stuffed generously with lobster meat, shrimp, and crawfish. Incredibly cheesy, flavorful with a spicy Cajun seasoning kick! YESSS LAWD!

Warning: Dangerously delicious!
Serving: 21 eggrolls

Equipment:
Large pan or skillet, 2 large mixing bowl, spatula or large spoon, small bowl, basting brush, fork,
cutting board, metal tongs, paper towel, large serving platter.

Prep time: 30 minutes
Cook time: 30 minutes
Total time: 1 hour

Ingredients

For the lobster tails:
- 4 lobster tails, raw
- 1 Tbsp cooking oil
- 1 tsp Cajun seasoning
- 1/4 tsp Blackened Old Bay Seasoning

For the shrimp:
- 1/2-pound shrimp, raw, cleaned, tails off, chopped into pieces
- 1/4 tsp Cajun seasoning
- 1 Tbsp cooking oil

For stuffing:
- 1 cup white rice, cooked
- 1-pound cooked crawfish tails, cooked, cleaned
- 4 garlic cloves*, minced
- 1 small red onion, chopped very fine
- 2 Tbsp Belay & Bell Smokehouse Rub, sweet and spicy

- 1 Tbsp Zatarain's Creole Seasoning
- 2-3 scallions, chopped
- 1/3 cup cheddar cheese, shredded
- Eggs Roll Wraps 1 lb. pack
- 2 eggs
- 1 cup cooking oil

For the dipping sauce:
- 1 bottle Valley Ranch dressing
- 2 Tbsp honey
- 2 tsp Louisiana Hot Sauce, original

Direction

For the lobster tails:
- Thaw out lobster tails if frozen. Then you want to crack your lobster tail open.
- Take the kitchen shears, and cut along the top of the shell, just a little underneath. You don't want to cut into the lobster meat! Run your fingers underneath the lobster tail between the meat and the shell to loosen it. Remove all dirt, veins, and rinse with water if needed.
- Using your fingers, gently open up the shell and pop the meat out of the shell.
- Slice lobster tails and cut them into small pieces.
- Preheat the large skillet with oil.
- Add chopped lobster pieces and sprinkle them with Cajun and Old Bay Seasonings.
- Cook on medium heat for 3-4 minutes, then remove the lobster meat and set them aside.

For the shrimp:
- Add cooking oil and shrimp to clean pan, sprinkle with Cajun seasoning. Cook for 2 minutes, stirring on high heat.

For the dipping sauce:
- In a small bowl, mix Valley Ranch dressing with honey and Louisiana Hot Sauce. Set aside.

For the stuffing:
- In a large bowl, add cooked rice, crawfish, lobster tails, shrimp, minced garlic, red onion, Belay & Bell Smokehouse Rub, Zatarain's Creole Seasoning, scallions, and cheese. Mix well!

Assemble:
- In a small bowl, crack the eggs open and whisk them with a fork.
- Lay egg roll wraps plat on a cutting board, brush the corners with beaten eggs.
- Place about ¼ cup of stuffing in the middle, take the wrap's back corner, and fold it over the stuffing. Then take the other sides, and fold it over like an envelope. And then roll it over.
- Repeat with all stuffing and egg rolls.
- Preheat the cooking oil on a large pan. Place rolls and cook them on medium-high for about 2 minutes on each side at most.
- Remove egg rolls from the pan and lay them on a paper towel to drain any excess fat.

Repeat with remaining rolls.
- Once egg rolls are done, place them on a serving platter with a side of dipping sauce!

Enjoy!

Note:
Minced garlic: you can mince 4 large garlic cloves or use 2 Tbsp Spice Worlds Minced Garlic Squeeze brand.

Smoked Cajun Crab Dip

Ok so BOOM this dip is addicting! Preparing this is as easy as 1-2-3! The jumbo lump crab meat and gourmet cheeses combine effortlessly to be the stars of this show! Yesss Lawd!

Serving: 8-10
Equipment: iron skillet, large bowl
Prep time: 10 minutes
Cook time: 30 minutes
Total time: 40 minutes

Ingredients

- 8 oz. whipped cream cheese
- ½ cup mayonnaise
- ½ cup sour cream
- ½ bag of spinach, chopped
- 1 tbsp olive oil
- 1 can of jumbo lump crab or crab claw
- ½ block Gruyere cheese
- ½ block Asiago cheese
- ½ block Smoked Gouda cheese
- 2 basil leaves, finely chopped
- 2 tsp minced garlic
- 2 tbsp Cajun seasoning, unsalted
- 1 tbsp Cajun seasoning, salted
- 2 tsp liquid smoke
- 2 tsp Louisiana Hot Sauce
- 2 tsp Worcestershire Sauce
- 1-2 tbsp smoked paprika
- 1-2 tbsp garlic powder
- 1-2 tbsp minced onion

Direction

- Preheat cast-iron skillet with oil over medium heat.
- Add spinach and cook it until tender for about 3-5 minutes.
- Shred or grate Gruyere, Asiago, and smoked Gouda cheese.
- Add 1/2 of each cheese into a large bowl, and mix all remaining ingredients for the dip.
- Preheat oven to 400 degrees Fahrenheit.
- Line cast iron skillet with cooking spray, then add mixture and top with remaining cheeses.
- Lightly sprinkle paprika on top of cheeses for extra added color.
- Bake spinach dip uncovered at 400F for 20-25 minutes.
- Serve with tortilla chips and enjoy!

Buffalo Lemon Pepper Salmon Tenders

If you are like me and grew up on a bags of frozen fish sticks, get excited about this recipe! Try my homemade Buffalo Lemon Pepper Salmon Tenders, a.k.a. Gourmet Fish Sticks! They are deliciously crispy, simple to prepare, and packed with flavors! Serve them with your favorite sides or as an appetizer!

Serving: 4

Equipment: 1 large bowl, 1 small bowl, 1 medium bowl, large skillet, wax paper

Prep time: 40 minutes
Cook time: 15 minutes
Total time: 55 minutes

Ingredients

For the fish:
- 2 pounds salmon fillet, defrosted, sliced into 1.5-2 inch pieces
- 1 cup buttermilk
- 1 Tbsp Green Pepper Cholula Hot sauce
- 1 Tbsp smoked paprika
- 1 tsp garlic powder
- 1 tsp onion powder
- 2 tsp Cajun seasoning, unsalted
- 1 tsp Tony Creole seasoning, salted
- 2 eggs
- 1 cup cooking oil

For the dry coating:
- 1 cup white flour
- 1 cup bread crumbs
- 2 tsp Cajun seasoning, unsalted
- 1/4 tsp smoked paprika
- 1/4 tsp garlic powder
- 1/4 tsp onion powder
- 1/4 tsp Tony Creole seasoning, salted
- 1 tsp McCormick Salt Free Garlic & Herbs Seasoning

For the lemon pepper sauce:
- 1 Tbsp favorite hot sauce
- 1 Tbsp MrsDash seasoning, Lemon Pepper
- 1/4 cup melted butter

For the dipping sauce:
- 1/4 cup store-bought cilantro paste*
- 1 Tbsp jalapeno paste*
- 2 Tbsp mayo
- 1/4 cup buttermilk
- 1 Tbsp Hidden Valley Ranch seasoning (optional)

Direction

For the fish:
- Place salmon fillets into a large bowl and season with buttermilk, hot sauce, smoked paprika, Cajun seasoning, eggs, Tony Creole seasoning, garlic, and onion powder.
- Using your hands, mix everything very well.
- Refrigerate for at least 25-30 minutes.
- Prepare the rest of the ingredients.

For the dry coating:
- In a large bowl, stir all ingredients for the dry coating. Set aside.

For the lemon pepper sauce:
- In a small bowl, whisk the melted butter with hot sauce and MrsDash seasoning. Set aside.

For the dipping sauce:
- In a medium bowl, stir all ingredients for the dipping sauce. Set aside.

Prepare the fish:
- Preheat large skillet on medium heat with cooking oil.
- Dip salmon fillets in a dry coating on all sides. Carefully place them into the hot oil and fry for 3-4 minutes on each side or until golden brown. Repeat with all fillets.

To serve:
- Serve with dipping sauce on a side.

Note:

McCormick Salt-Free Garlic & Herbs Seasoning: if you don't have it, use an equal amount of each (pinch): oregano, parsley, rosemary, dried basil, red pepper flakes, onion powder, and smoked paprika.

Store-bought cilantro paste: to substitute, add 1/3 cup of cilantro with 2 Tbsp of oil in a small blender, puree for 30 seconds. Season with salt to taste.

Replace jalapeno paste* with 1/4 small Jalapeno pepper (sliced very thin, seeds removed).

Blackened Salmon Deviled Eggs

The appetizer you never knew you needed! Here's a creative spin on a classic. These Blackened Salmon Deviled Eggs are perfect for entertaining! They have a delicious smoky filling, topped with blackened salmon and hot honey sauce! What are you waiting for? Let's get it!

Serving: 24

Equipment:

Large pot, large bowl, medium skillet, medium bowl, medium Ziploc bag, kitchen scissors, large serving platter.

Prep time: 20 minutes
Cook time: 15 minutes
Total time: 35 minutes

Ingredients

For the salmon:

- 1 pound fresh salmon fillet, skinless, boneless
- 1 Tbsp cooking oil
- 1 Tbsp Cajun seasoning, unsalted
- 1 Tbsp garlic powder
- 1 Tbsp onion powder
- 1 Tbsp Blackened Old Bay Seasoning
- 1 Tbsp smoked paprika
- 1/4 tsp fine sea salt

For the eggs:
- 12 eggs (one dozen)
- 4 Tbsp "Truff" Black Truffle infused mayonnaise
- 2 tsp garlic powder
- 1 tsp yellow mustard
- 1 tsp smoked paprika
- 2 tsp sweet relish
- 1/4 tsp Blackened Old Bay
- 1/2 tsp onion powder
- 1/2 tsp your favorite hot sauce
- 1/4 tsp Cajun seasoning
- 2-3 drops hickory liquid smoke
- 1/2 tsp Worcestershire sauce.
- 6 Tbsp Frank's Red Hot - Honey Garlic sauce

Direction

For the eggs:
- Place eggs in a large pot and cover with cold water by 1 inch. Bring to boil, then simmer for 10 minutes, covered with lead.
- Transfer cooked eggs to a large bowl with cold water and ice cubes and chill until needed.

For the salmon:
- Preheat medium skillet with cooking oil.
- Add salmon and cook for 5 minutes on medium heat on each side.
- Remove from the pan and flake with a fork into 1-1.5 inch pieces. Set them aside.

For the eggs:
- Peel the eggs, and cut them lengthwise.
- Remove the egg yolks and empty them into a medium bowl.
- Add truffle mayo, garlic, mustard, smoked paprika, sweet relish, Old Bay, Cajun seasoning, hot sauce, garlic and onion powder, liquid smoke, and Worcestershire sauce. Stir until combined. Spoon eggs stuffing into a medium-sized Ziploc bag, and cut a corner just a little.

Assemble:
- Place egg halves on a large serving platter, and squeeze the filling inside of each egg.
- Top with salmon pieces and drizzle with honey garlic sauce.
- Dig in!

Cajun Caesar Salad Boats

One thing I understand the most in my craft is that balance is key! With all the savory meals I prepare, it's just as important to throw in some healthy alternatives as well. This salad recipe is just the right meal to get the job done.

These lightened-up Cajun Caesar Salad Boats are served in individual pieces of Romaine lettuce stalks. Delicious update to a classic Caesar salad with my own Southern twist added! Yes Lawd!

Serving: 2
Equipment: baking pan, small bowl, medium bowl, skillet, 2 large flat servings plates
Prep time: 10 minutes
Cook time: 15 minutes
Total time: 20 minutes

Ingredients

For the croutons:
- 1/2 French bread, cubed into bite-size pieces
- 2 tsp Cajun seasoning, unsalted
- 2 Tbsp cooking oil
- 1/4 tsp salt
- 1 tsp garlic powder

For the chicken
- 1 medium chicken breast, boneless, skinless, cubed into bite-size pieces
- 1/4 tsp Tony Creole seasoning
- 1/2 smoked paprika
- 1/4 tsp Blackened Old Bay Seasoning
- Cooking spray

To assemble:
- 4 large romaine lettuce leaves
- 1/4 cup your favorite Caesar dressing
- 1/4 tsp garlic powder
- Pinch black pepper
- 4 lemon wedges
- 1/4 cup freshly grated Parmesan cheese

Direction

For the croutons:
- Preheat the oven to 400F.
- Toss bread with Cajun seasoning, cooking oil, salt, and garlic powder in a baking pan.
- Bake it until golden brown for 7-8 minutes. Alternatively, you can use the air fryer and cook the croutons for 5 minutes.
- Remove the croutons from the oven and set them aside in a separate bowl.

For the chicken:
- Place the chicken breast in a medium bowl and season it with Tony Creole seasoning, smoked paprika, and Blackened Old Bay Seasoning. Mix well, making sure the chicken pieces are evenly coated.
- Spray the skillet with cooking oil spray and preheat it on medium heat.
- Add chicken to the skillet and cook for 6-8 minutes, stirring.

To assemble:
- Place romaine lettuce leaves on large flat serving plates; two each.
- Add chicken and croutons evenly horizontally on each lettuce leaf.
- Drizzle them with your favorite Caesar dressing and lemon juice.
- Then, sprinkle with garlic powder and black pepper.
- Top with freshly grated Parmesan cheese, and serve immediately! YUM!

Fried Green Tomatoes with Bacon Jam Dip

Ok so I know not everyone is huge fan of tomatoes but I'm here to tell you that these Fried Green Tomatoes with Bacon Jam Dip will change your mind. Trust me, my tomatoes are golden fried, crispy, salty with a hint of southern soul! I bet this will become one of your favorites!

Serving: 8

Equipment: whisk, 2 medium bowls, flat medium plate, cutting board, large skillet, paper towel

Prep time: 30 minutes
Cook time: 1 hour
Total time: 1 hour 30 minutes

Ingredients

For the tomatoes:
- 6 large firm green tomatoes
- 1 cup mayo
- 1/2 cup whole milk
- 2.5-3 cups plain panko breadcrumbs
- 1 cup cornstarch
- 3 Tbsp Cajun seasoning, salted
- 1 tsp smoked paprika
- 1 Tbsp garlic powder
- 2 tsp onion powder
- 1/2 cup cooking oil

For the bacon jam dip:
- 4 slices thick bacon
- 1 medium onion, sliced thin
- 1/4 cup brown sugar
- 4 Tbsp maple syrup
- 1/4 tsp smoked paprika
- 1/2 cup water

To serve:
- 1/4 cup mayo
- 1/4 cup sour cream

Direction

Prepare the dip first.

For the bacon jam dip:
- Preheat a large skillet and add bacon.
- Cook it for about 4 minutes on each side over medium heat.
- Remove bacon from the skillet and lay it on a paper towel to drain any excess fat.
- Chop the bacon into bite-sized pieces.
- Using the same skillet and leftover bacon grease, fry sliced onion for about 5-6 minutes.
- Next, add brown sugar, maple syrup, smoked paprika, and water. Stir and bring the mixture to a boil.
- Reduce the heat. Add bacon pieces and allow the jam mixture to simmer for 45 minutes to one hour. Stir every 8-10 minutes. When it's done, it should have a slightly gooey consistency.
- Remove jam from the heat, and transfer it into a bowl. Allow the mixture to cool down while frying the tomatoes.

For the tomatoes:
- Using a medium bowl, whisk mayo with milk. Set aside.
- Mix panko breadcrumbs with Cajun seasoning, smoked paprika, garlic, and onion powder in a separate medium bowl. Set aside.
- Add cornstarch to a flat medium plate. Set aside.
- Next, slice green tomatoes into 1 ½ inch thick slices.
- Preheat the skillet with oil over medium-high heat.
- Dip tomato slice into a cornstarch, coating all sides.
- Then dip it into a mayo/milk mixture.
- The last, dip it into panko/spices mixture. Make sure to coat all sides.
- Repeat with all slices.
- Carefully place coated tomatoes in hot oil and fry for 2 minutes on each side (until each side is golden color). Don't overcrowd the skillet. Repeat with all tomatoes.
- Allow them to rest on a cutting board, covered with a paper towel to drain excess grease.

To serve:
- Transfer bacon jam into a small blender. Blend in with mayo and sour cream.
- Serve fried tomatoes with bacon jam dip! Delicious!

Garlic Parmesan Lobster Tails

This Garlic Parmesan Lobster Tails recipe went VIRAL on Instagram and without a doubt I know they'll go viral in your home amongst your family! Made with large meaty lobster tails topped with a buttery smoky sauce and fresh Parmesan cheese.

This recipe is quick and easy. These lobster tails are made in the oven in just 15 minutes! Yes Lawd!

Serving: 4 portions

Equipment:
Kitchen shears, large skillet, medium bowl, large baking tray, basting brush or spatula, 4 large serving plates.

Prep time: 15 minutes

Cook time: 15-20 minutes

Total time: 30-35 minutes

Ingredients

- 8 large lobster tails

For the butter sauce:
- 2 sticks of butter
- 2 Tbsp minced garlic*
- 1/2 tsp garlic powder
- 1 tsp Old Bay seasoning

- 1/2 tsp smoked paprika
- 1/4 tsp garlic pepper
- Juice from the half of the lemon
- 1/3 cup Parmesan cheese
- 1/2 tsp liquid hickory smoke
- •1/4 cup minced fresh parsley

Direction

- Thaw out lobster tails if frozen. Then you want to crack your lobster tail open.
- Take the kitchen shears, and cut along the top of the shell, just a little underneath, leaving the tail fan intact. You don't want to cut into the lobster meat! Cut it almost to the back of the tail.
- Run your fingers underneath the lobster tail between the meat and the shell to loosen it. Remove all dirt, veins, and rinse with water if needed.
- Using your fingers, gently open up the shell and pop the meat slightly out.
- Preheat the large skillet on medium heat and add butter.
- Once butter is melted, add minced garlic, garlic powder, Old Bay seasoning, smoked paprika, and garlic pepper. Stir in and drizzle with lemon juice.
- Whisk the sauce, and simmer it for a few minutes until butter bubbling very lightly.
- Remove from the heat and add hickory smoke, minced parsley, and Parmesan cheese.
- Now, it's time to cook the lobster tails.
- Arrange the tails on a large baking pan. Using the spatula, brush them with half of the butter sauce over the lobster tails.
- Preheat the oven to 400 degrees F.
- Place lobster tails into the oven for 15-20 minutes.
- Remove tails from the oven, drizzle with the remaining butter sauce and serve immediately!
- Enjoy these buttery, garlicky, smoky, succulent tails paired with my seafood mac and cheese and lamb chops.

Note:
Minced garlic: you can mince 2 large garlic cloves or use 1 Tbsp Spice Worlds Minced Garlic Squeeze brand.

Jalapeno Lime Corn on the Cob

If you know me then you know I'm not the biggest fan of elote but THIS RIGHT HERE is my spin and it's bussin! This recipe is quick, easy, and counter slapping good! My Jalapeno Lime Corn on the Cob has the perfect combination of butter, spicy peppers, lime, and parmesan cheese. Enjoy this as an easy side dish any day of the week.
SO GOOD!

Serving: 8
Equipment: baking pan, large bowl, tongs, large flat platter for serving
Prep time: 5 minutes
Cook time: 25 minutes
Total time: 30 minutes

Ingredients

- 8 ears of corn, cleaned
- 1 stick butter
- 1 Tbsp jalapeño pepper paste*
- 1 Tbsp Tajin seasoning*
- 1 Tbsp Hidden Valley Ranch Seasoning
- 2 tsp minced garlic*
- 1/2 cup Parmesan and cotija cheese, shredded
- 1 lime, juiced
- Parsley (garnish only)

Direction

- Wrap each ear of corn with aluminum foil
- Preheat oven to 425F and bake for 25 minutes.
- Add butter, jalapeño pepper paste, Tajin, ranch seasoning, and garlic in a large bowl. Microwave this mixture for 10-12 seconds or melt in a small saucepan on medium-low for 5-7 minutes.
- Next, whisk it with a fork and set aside.
- Carefully remove the corn from the oven and lay it on a flat serving platter.
- Brush each corn with the butter sauce on both sides.
- Sprinkle them generously with shredded Parmesan and cotija cheese, and drizzle with lime juice.
- Garnish with parsley, serve, and enjoy!

Note:
Jalapeño pepper paste: if you don't have it, simply trip the step ends of one small jalapeño. Use gloves! Cut the pepper in half, removing the seeds. Chop it into tiny pieces.
Minced garlic: you can mince 1 small garlic clove or use 2 tsp Spice Worlds Minced Garlic Squeeze brand.
Tajin seasoning: if you don't have it, use 1/4 tsp of salt and 1/4 tsp of dried red chili pepper flakes.

Boudin Stuffed Biscuits

Listen!! Yes! Yes! Yes! If you're not familiar with Boudin there's no need fret. You'll be obsessed with these biscuits. It's a super easy Louisiana flavors inspired recipe that will be on your table in under 25 minutes!

Serving: 6 biscuits

Equipment: medium skillet, potato masher, ice-cream scoop, baking sheet or pan, medium microwavable bowl

Prep time: 10 minutes
Cook time: 15 minutes
Total time: 25 minutes

Ingredients

For the biscuits:
- 2 Boudin sausages
- 1 small onion, chopped
- 1/4 cup Parmesan cheese, shredded
- 2 tsp Louisiana Hot Sauce, original
- 1 package Betty Crocker Bisquick Buttermilk Mix
- •Cooking spray

For the sauce:
- 1/2 stick butter, unsalted, room temperature
- 1 Tbsp Old Bay Seasoning
- 2 tsp Cajun seasoning, unsalted
- 1 tsp parsley
- 2 tsp Louisiana Hot Sauce, original

Direction

- First, take the skin off the boudin sausages.
- Preheat the skillet, and cook boudin until they are browned for 5 minutes on medium heat.

- Then mash the sausages with a potato masher, and add chopped onion, cheese, and hot sauce. Mix it well and sauté the boudin for 3-4 more minutes.
- Please remove it from the heat and set it aside.
- Spray the baking sheet with a cooking spray.
- Mix the Betty Crocker Bisquick Buttermilk Mix with water, according to the package directions.
- Wet your hands. Using the ice cream scoop, scoop the biscuit batter in your hand. Next, place about 3 Tbsp of boudin in the middle of the biscuit. Pinch the dough sides until they are sealed.
- Place the finished biscuit on a baking sheet and repeat with the remaining ingredients to make 5 more stuffed biscuits.
- Cook them on 450F until they are golden brown, about 10 minutes.

For the butter sauce:
- Take a medium microwavable bowl and place butter into it. Season it with Old Bay, Cajun, parsley, and hot sauce.
- Microwave the butter for 5-10 seconds.

To assemble:
- Brushed the finished biscuits with melted butter sauce and serve warm.

Surf and Turf Burger

Now I'll start by saying this fancy burger is not for any ole guest! Bring out these boujee burgers for your elite guest when you're trying to showcase your diverse pallet. These melt-in-your mouth Surf & Turf Burgers are made with seasoned, juicy Wagyu beef and premium Jumbo Lump crabmeat. They are served on toasted Brioche buns, topped with caramelized onions and smoky, spicy truffle-infused sauce. Let's get ready for a luxury burger experience! Yes Lawd!

Serving:
4 burgers 6-ounces each

Equipment:
Large pan or skillet, 1 large mixing bowl, spatula, small bowl, 4 serving plates.

Prep time: 20 minutes
Cook time: 10 minutes
Total time: 30 minutes

Ingredients

For the burgers:
- 1 pound ground Wagyu beef*
- 8 oz Jumbo Lump Crab, ready to eat crab meat
- 1 tsp Old Bay Seasoning Garlic & Herbs
- 1 Tbsp Belay & Bell Smokehouse Rub
- 1/4 tsp pink Himalayan sea salt
- 1/4 tsp fine black pepper
- 3 Tbsp President Spreadable Brie cheese

For the sauce:
- 4 Tbsp "Truff" Black Truffle infused mayonnaise
- 1 tsp yellow mustard
- 2 minced garlic cloves*
- ¼ tsp Cajun seasoning
- ¼ tsp hot sauce

- 3 drops liquid hickory smoke

To assemble:
- 2 Tbsp cooking oil
- 1 large yellow onion, chopped
- 4 Brioche buns
- A handful of fresh spinach or arugula
- 1 medium tomato, sliced thick

Direction

For the burgers:
- In a large pan or skillet, heat the cooking oil on medium. Add roughly chopped yellow onions. Cook them for 5 minutes until they are tender, golden in color, and flagrant. Remove the onions from the heat and set them aside.
- In a large bowl, add all ingredients for the burgers and hand mix them.
- Divide the ground beef mixture into 4 equal portions, 6-ounces each. Place burgers in a large preheated large pan or skillet. Cook them on medium to medium-high heat, 4-5 minutes on each side. Be careful, don't overcook the burgers!
- Remove cooked burgers from the pan and allow them to rest while you are preparing the sauce and toasting Brioche buns.
- Place burgers buns on preheat skillet and toast them for 2 minutes on medium heat.

For the sauce:
- In a small bowl, whisk in all ingredients for the sauce.

Assemble:
- Spread the sauce over the toasted Brioche bun and top with fresh spinach or arugula. Add tomato slice, burger, and top with onions. The final touch, drizzle it with sauce and cover with another bun!
- Dig in and enjoy!

Note:
- Wagyu beef*: for the lower budget version, you can use 80/20 ground chuck meat. Its 80% lean meat & 20% fat, the ideal lean-to-fat ratio for super juicy burgers.
- Garlic cloves*: you can mince 2 garlic cloves or use 1 Tbsp Spice Worlds Minced Garlic Squeeze brand.

Seafood Melt

Take the traditional grilled cheese sandwich to new heights by turning it into the most incredible sandwich you'll ever make! Crabmeat, salmon, cheese, and Cajun seasonings are such a glorious combo!
Is there anything more comforting than a toasty smoked Gouda, Italian blend cheese cooked to perfection with seafood whipped cream?!
This is a gourmet sandwich!

Serving:
2 large sandwiches

Equipment:
baking sheet, medium bowl, ice-cream scoop, skillet, cooking tongs

Prep time: 10 minutes
Cook time: 10 minutes
Total time: 20 minutes

Ingredients

For the cream cheese filling:
- 2 scoops of whipped cream cheese
- 1/4 tsp smoked paprika
- 1/4 tsp garlic powder
- 1 tsp minced garlic
- 1/4 tsp Tony Creole seasoning
- 1/4 cup crabmeat, cooked

For the fish:
- 4-5oz small pieces of salmon, skin free
- 1 tsp Tony Creole seasoning
- 1/2 tsp garlic powder
- 1/2 tsp smoked paprika
- Cooking oil

To assemble:
- 4 slices of sliced Sourdough or Brioche bread
- 1/4 cup Gouda cheese, shredded or sliced
- 1/4 cup Italian blend cheese, shredded
- 1/4 cup mayonnaise
- 2 Tbsp butter, unsalted

Direction

For the cream cheese filling:
- In a medium bowl, add whipped cream cheese, smoked paprika, garlic powder, minced garlic, Tony Creole seasoning and crabmeat.
- Mix it with the fork to incorporate. Set aside.

For the salmon:
- Season the salmon with Tony Creole seasoning, garlic powder, and smoked paprika.
- Add cooking oil to the skillet and sear the fish for 3-4 minutes on each side.
- Place the salmon on a board and break it up with a fork or tongs into bite-sized pieces.

For the cream cheese filling (continue):
- Add flaked salmon to the cream cheese crab mixture, and fold everything to together.

To assemble:
- Place one slice of bread on a flat plate and sprinkle it with Gouda cheese. Then spoon in the seafood filling.
- Sprinkle the filling with an Italian cheese blend and cover it with the other slice of bread.
- Spread the mayo on a top slice.
- Take butter, add it to a skillet, and melt it down.
- Place the sandwich on a pan, mayo side up. Cook it on medium heat for 3 minutes.
- Carefully flit the sandwich and fry it for 3 more minutes.
- Repeat with another sandwich.
- Cut the sandwich diagonally before the serving!
- I can smell the clogged arteries, but we gonna have a good time! Enjoy!

Blackened Cod Sandwich

Love the fish sandwiches? Me too! Those toasty soft buns, Cajun seasoned Cod fillets, and the best easy sauce! Skip takeout and make this at home in under 15 minutes!

Serving: 2

Equipment: large bowl, skillet, small bowl

Prep time: 5 minutes

Cook time: 10 minutes

Total time: 15 minutes

Ingredients

For the fish:
- 2 large Cod fillets, defrosted
- 1 tsp Blackened Old Bay Seasoning
- 1 Tbsp minced garlic*
- 1 Tbsp onion powder
- 1 tsp smoked paprika
- 2 Tbsp cooking oil

For the sauce:
- 1 Tbsp mayo
- 2 tsp Dijon mustard
- 2 tsp fresh dill, minced
- 2 tsp favorite hot sauce

To assemble:
- 4 buns
- 4 romaine lettuce leaves
- 1 small tomato, sliced

Direction

For the fish:
- Rub the fish with Old Bay Seasoning, minced garlic, onion powder, and smoked paprika.
- Preheat large skillet over medium heat with cooking oil.
- Fry the fish for 4-5 minutes on each side.
- Remove it from the pan and set aside.

For the sauce:
- In a small bowl whisk all ingredients.

To assemble:
- Toast the buns.
- Spread the sauce over the buns, top with fried fish, lettuce, and tomato. Your easy delicious sandwich is ready! Enjoy!

Note:

Minced garlic: you can mince 1 large garlic cloves or use 1 Tbsp Spice Worlds Minced Garlic Squeeze brand.

Hot Honey Salmon Club

Beautiful golden brown and crispy salmon on brioche buns, topped with hot honey sauce. It's a rich and flavorful combination that everyone will love!

Serving: 4

Equipment: large bowl, deep glass container, fork, large skillet, tongs for frying, 2 small bowls, cooking brush.

Prep time: 10 minutes
Cook time: 15 minutes
Total time: 25 minutes

Ingredients

- 1 ½ pound salmon fillets, skinless
- 2 eggs
- 2 Tbsp yellow mustard
- 1/2 cup cooking oil
- 4 brioche buns, toasted
- 1/2 cup shredded lettuce
- 1 medium tomato, sliced thick
- 4 onion slices
- 8 bacon slices, fried to desired crispiness

For the salmon spices:

- 2 Tbsp Tony's Cajun seasoning, unsalted
- 1 Tbsp Slap Ya Mama Cajun seasoning
- 1 Tbsp smoked paprika

For the dry batter:

- 1 cup potato starch
- 1 cup corn starch
- 1 Tbsp Tony's Cajun seasoning, unsalted
- 1 Tbsp Slap Ya Mama Cajun seasoning
- 1 Tbsp smoked paprika

For the mayo sauce:

- 1 Tbsp mayo
- 1 Tbsp sour cream
- 2 Tbsp fresh lemon juice

- 2 tsp minced garlic
- 1 tsp lemon pepper
- Handful fresh parsley, chopped

For the hot honey sauce:
- 1 Tbsp Buffalo hot sauce
- 1/4 cup honey

Direction

- In a large bowl, place salmon fillets and add salmon spices to it. Add eggs and mustard to the bowl.
- Using your hands, incorporate all ingredients, making sure all salmon fillets are covered well. Set aside and prepare the dry batter.

For the dry batter:
- In a glass container, add all ingredients for the batter, and whisk well with a fork.

Prepare the salmon:
- Take the salmon and dip it into the dry batter on both sides. Shake any excess batter.

Repeat with all fillets.
- Preheat the skillet with cooking oil. Carefully place the salmon fillet into the hot oil. Fry the fish on medium-high heat for 3-4 minutes on each side.
- Remove the salmon using a spatula or tongs, and place them on a paper towel. This will drain any excess oil, making them even crispier.

For the mayo sauce:
- In a small bowl, stir all ingredients for the sauce. Set it aside.

For the hot honey sauce:
- In a separate small bowl, whisk honey with hot sauce. Set aside.

To assemble:
- Brush salmon fillets with honey sauce.
- Spread the mayo sauce over the buns on all sides. Sprinkle one side with shredded lettuce, add a slice of fresh onion and tomato.
- Top with salmon and two bacon slices for each bun.
- Cover with a second bun and enjoy!

Cornbread Pot Roast Sliders

This recipe is simple and absolutely delicious! A combination of sweet, moist cornbread with tender and juicy pot roast transforms an affordable meal into a mouthwatering comfort food
dinner!

Serving: 8-10

Equipment:
Large bowl, cast iron skillet, large slow cooker or crock pot, large cooking tray, spatula

Prep time: 30 minutes
Cook time: 8 hours minutes
Total time: 8.5 hours

Ingredients

- 8 large potatoes, cut in quarters
- 2 large carrots, cut into large chunks
- 2 medium onion, sliced thick

For the meat:
- • 1 pound boneless chuck roast
- 1 Tbsp pink Himalayan sea salt
- 1/2 tsp fine black pepper
- 1 Tbsp onion powder
- 1 Tbsp garlic powder
- 1/4 cup Valley Ranch seasoning
- 10 oz beef broth
- 1 tsp concentrated beef bouillon
- 10 oz dry red wine
- 2 tsp Worcestershire sauce
- 1/4 cup corn starch sifted

For the cornbread:
- 3 Jiffy Corn Muffin mix
- 3 eggs
- 1 cup whole milk
- 1/3 favorite cheese, shredded
- Cooking spray
- 3 Tbsp honey

Assemble:
- 1 pound fresh Mozzarella cheese, sliced thick
- To taste Louisiana Hot Sauce, original

Direction

For the meat:
- Prepare the roast. Season the meat with sea salt, black pepper, onion powder, garlic powder, and Valley Ranch seasoning in a large bowl. Rub them into the meat well.
- Preheat the cast iron and sear the roast for 4 minutes on each side over medium heat. This will help the roast to develop a nice crust and lock the flavors with juices in!
- Remove the meat from the skillet.
- Place the potatoes on the bottom of the slow cooker. Top them with seared roast and pour beef broth over them.
- Add concentrated beef bouillon and Worcestershire sauce. Stir.
- Gently pour red wine over the roast. This will not make the meat sweet, and it will help to tenderize the roast!
- Sprinkle with sifted corn starch and stir it, just a little.
- Cook pot roast for 5 hours on low heat. After that add carrots and potatoes, and cook for 3 more hours.

For the cornbread:
- To prepare the cornbread, follow the instruction on the back of the Jiffy Corn Muffin mixes.
- Spray a large cooking tray with oil.
- Pour the cornbread mix into this baking dish/tray, and place it into the oven for 20-30 minutes.
- Remove the bread from the oven, and drizzle it with honey.
- Please put it back into the oven for another 5 minutes.
- Once the cornbread is done, take it out of the oven and allow it to rest while the roast is cooking.

Assemble:
- • Slice the cornbread into squares and arrange it on plates. Top it with fresh Mozzarella cheese and hot roast. Drizzle with Louisiana Hot Sauce and juices from the roast! Dig in!

The LOX Melt

A must-have serious soul food sandwich that's guaranteed to excite your taste buds! Extra-rich tasting oxtail meat reminds most people of delicious short ribs or pot roast. Combines with succulent lobsters tail meat and jerk sauce, this recipe creates an incredible top-notch sandwich experience! Must try!

Serving: 6

Equipment
large bowl, plastic wrap, large cast iron skillet, kitchen shears, large skillet.

Prep time: 24 hours
Cook time: 2.5-3 hours

Ingredients

- 2 pounds oxtail, washed, fat trimmed
- 2 Tbsp olive oil
- 1 ½ cup red wine
- 1/2 sliced habanero pepper
- 2 sweet bell peppers, sliced
- 1 medium onion, diced
- 2 cup beef broth
- 2 Tbsp mayo
- 2 Tbsp Jerk seasoning
- 6 lobster tails
- 1/2 stick butter
- 12 sourdough bread slices
- 2 cups shredded Italian or Provolone cheese

For the oxtail marinade seasoning:
- 1 Tbsp Worcestershire sauce
- 1 Tbsp smoked paprika
- 2 tsp liquid hickory smoke
- 2 Tbsp fine black pepper
- 2 Tbsp garlic powder
- 2 Tbsp onion powder
- 2 Tbsp ground cumin
- 1 Tbsp garlic peppers seasoning
- 1 Tbsp dried thyme seasoning

Direction

- In a large bowl, add oxtail and all seasoning for it. Using your hands, mix the meat with all oxtail marinade seasoning.
- Cover the bowl with plastic wrap, and refrigerate for at least 2 hours. The best would be overnight or for 24 hours!
- After the oxtails are marinated, start cooking them.
- Preheat the large cast-iron skillet with olive oil over medium-high heat. Add marinated oxtails and sear them for 4 minutes on each side.
- When oxtails are seared: deglaze the skillet. Add red wine, sliced habanero pepper, bell peppers, onion, and glaze them for 5 minutes.
- Add beef broth to a skillet.
- Preheat oven to 350F and add iron skillet with oxtails, vegetables, and broth into it. Cook it for 2.5-3 hours. The meat should be tender once they are done.

Prepare the jerk mayo:
In a small bowl, whisk mayo with jerk seasoning. Set aside.

For the lobsters:
- Thaw out lobster tails if frozen. Then you want to crack your lobster tail open.
- Take the kitchen shears, and cut along the top of the shell, just a little underneath, leaving the tail fan intact. You don't want to cut into the lobster meat! Cut it almost to the back of the tail.
- Run your fingers underneath the lobster tail between the meat and the shell to loosen it. Remove all dirt, veins, and rinse with water if needed.
- Using your fingers, gently open up the shell and pop the meat out.
- Preheat the large skillet on medium heat with butter. Add lobster tails and cook them for 2 minutes on each side.
- Take them out of the skillet and let them rest.

To assemble:
- Spread jerk mayo on all sides of the bread, top with cheese, shredded oxtail meal, and chopped lobster tail meat.
- Pour about 2-3Tbsp of oxtail juice over the sandwich.
- Top with more cheese and another bread slice.
- Press gently and toast on a skillet over medium heat for 3 minutes on each side.

Loaded Southern Seafood Grits

Seafood Grits is a southern classic, and as you know me by now, I always put an extra flavor spin on any recipe I make!
It's amazingly creamy and loaded with crab legs, crawfish, and shrimp.
Let's get started, and I got you covered!

Serving: 6

Equipment:
Medium bowl, large pot, whisk, 6 large plates for serving

Prep time: 20 minutes
Cook time: 30 minutes
Total time: 50 minutes

Ingredients

- 1 pound crab legs, cleaned, cooked
- 1/2-pound crawfish meat, cleaned and cooked

For the shrimp:
- 2 tsp Tony Creole seasoning
- 1 tsp McCormick Salt Free Garlic & Herbs
- 1 tsp Fiesta Garlic Pepper
- 1 Tbsp cooking oil

For the grits:
- 4 cups chicken stock
- 4 cups heavy cream
- 1 tsp Tony Creole seasoning
- 1 tsp McCormick Salt Free Garlic & Herbs
- 1/4 tsp smoked paprika
- 1/2 stick of butter
- 1/3 cup Gouda cheese, shredded
- 1/3 cup Gruyere cheese, shredded

For the peppers:
- 4 sweet bell peppers, sliced thin
- 2 cups chicken stock
- 1/3 cup white flour, sifted

Direction

For the shrimp:
- In a medium bowl, add raw shrimp, McCormick, and Fiesta Garlic Pepper seasoning. Mix well and set aside.
- Preheat a large pan with cooking oil. Add shrimp and them for 2 minutes on each side over medium heat. Remove shrimp from the stove and set them aside.

For the peppers:
- Place peppers on a large pan, and add chicken broth. Whisk well.
- Bring to a boil, then add sifted flour and whisk well.

Continue:
- Add cooked crawfish, crab legs, and shrimp to peppers. Stir everything up.

For the grits:
- Pour chicken stock and heavy cream into a large pot, and bring to a boil.
- Season with spices. Then add slowly add grit, one cup at a time. Whisk the grits as you add it in.
- Add butter and cheese, reduce heat to low.
- Continue cooking covered for about 15-20 minutes.

Assemble:
- Once grits are done, plate it carefully and top it with a seafood mixture. Done!

Jerk Chicken & Sweet Potato Cornbread Waffles

Spicy, sweet with a plenty of flavors and herbs. Try this easy air-fried chicken, sweet potato waffles made from scratch, and I am sure you will fall in love with this good recipe!!!

Serving: 2

Equipment: whisk, air fryer or oven, baking sheet, 2 medium bowls, waffle maker

Prep time: 20 minutes
Cook time: 30 minutes
Total time: 50 minutes

Ingredients

For the potatoes:
- 1 large sweet potato, peeled

For the chicken:
- 2 chicken thighs
- 1 bottle Tony Ingestible Marinade
- 1 Tbsp MrsDash seasoning, Caribbean citrus
- 1 Tbsp Jamaican allspice
- 2 tsp garlic powder
- 2 tsp onion powder
- 2 tsp Jerk sauce

For the waffles:
- 1 cup cornmeal
- 1 cup white flour
- 2 Tbsp white sugar
- Pinch salt
- 1 cup buttermilk
- 2 eggs
- 1/2 cup melted butter
- 1 tsp vanilla extract
- 2 tsp cinnamon
- Pinch nutmeg
- 1/4 cup brown sugar
- 2 Tbsp maple syrup

Direction

- Boil the potato until fork tender for about 30 minutes.
- When it's done, mash it and set it aside.

For the chicken:
- Place chicken thighs on cutting board and pat them dry with a paper towel. This will ensure their skin will become crispier during the cooking process.
- Assemble the injector that comes with the marinade.
- Inject the chicken all around the thighs. Use 1/2 injector for one leg.
- Next, run the skins of the hens with MrsDash seasoning, Jamaican allspice, Jerk sauce, garlic, and onion powder.
- Preheat air fryer to 360F
- Place chicken into the air-fryer buckets and cook it for 25 minutes.
- Flip halfway through.
- Remove the chicken legs, let them rest on a cutting board while you are preparing the waffles.

For the waffles:
- In a small bowl, mix dry ingredients: cornmeal, white flour, white sugar, salt, cinnamon, nutmeg, and brown sugar.
- In a separate bowl, whisk to incorporate: mashed potato, buttermilk, eggs, melted butter, vanilla extract, and maple syrup.
- Spray the waffle maker with cooking spray and preheat it.
- Pour about 1/2 cup into the waffle maker (or less, depending on the size of your waffle maker). Cook for 3-4 minutes.

To serve:
- Serve waffles with chicken, drizzled with maple syrup.

Brunchaholic

Breakfast for dinner, why not! Try my mouthwatering Brunchaholic recipe, and you'll never do French toast any other way! It features smoked sausages with Jack Daniel's French toast and cheesy garlic eggs on aside. It's hearty and delicious!

Serving: 6 portions
Equipment:
2 large bowls, fork or whisk, large skillet, 4 plates for serving
Prep time: 10 minutes
Cook time: 20 minutes
Total time: 30 minutes

Ingredients

For the custard:
- 4 large eggs
- 1 cup heavy whipping cream
- 1 shot Jack Daniel's Tennessee Honey
- 1 tsp vanilla extract
- 1 tsp nutmeg
- 1 Tbsp brown sugar
- 1 tsp cinnamon

For the scrambled eggs:
- 4 large eggs
- 1/4 cup fresh parmesan cheese
- 2 minced garlic cloves*
- 2 Tbsp heavy whipping cream
- 1/4 tsp fine black pepper

For the French toast:
- 2 smoked fully cooked sausages
- 1/2 loaf Brioche Cinnamon bread
- 2 Tbsp butter
- 1/4 tsp powdered sugar
- 2 Tbsp maple syrup

Direction

For the custard:
- In a large bowl, crack the eggs and add heavy cream, short of Jack, vanilla extract, nutmeg, brown sugar and cinnamon. Whisk it with a fork until everything is blended. Set aside.

For the scrambled eggs:
- In a separate large bowl, whisk eggs with fresh parmesan cheese, garlic cloves, whipping cream, and black pepper. Set aside.

For the sausages:
- Slice sausages in half, lengthwise. Place on a pan and fry for 3 minutes on each side. Set aside.

For the French toast:
- Clean the skillet from the sausage fat and leftovers.
- Preheat the clean pan with butter.
- Dip each bread slice into a custard mixture. Place on pan and cook on medium heat for 4 minutes on each side. Repeat with remaining bread slices. Set aside.
- Cook scrambled eggs on medium-low for 2-3 minutes.
- Arrange toasts on serving plates, add scrambled eggs and sausages. Sprinkle toast with powdered sugar and drizzle with maple syrup. Enjoy!

Note:
Minced garlic: you can mince 2 large garlic cloves or use 1 Tbsp Spice Worlds Minced Garlic Squeeze brand.

Seafood Fried Rice

If you are looking to make an authentic Asian-style recipe but want it to be low carb and healthy, this is for you!

One-pan super easy dish! It's loaded with shrimp, crawfish, broccoli, and cauliflower and spiced with good old seafood seasoning! Dinner fix in under 20 minutes!

Serving: 2

Equipment: large bowl, large skillet

Prep time: 5 minutes
Cook time: 10 minutes
Total time: 15 minutes

Ingredients

For the shrimp:

- 1 pound shrimp, cleaned, defrosted
- 1 tsp Old Bay Seasoning Garlic & Herbs
- 1 Tbsp Flawless Flavor Seafood Seasoning*
- 1 tsp onion powder
- 1 tsp garlic powder
- 1/2 tsp smoked paprika
- 1 bag cauliflower rice
- 2 cups broccoli florets
- 1 Tbsp sesame oil
- 3 eggs
- 1 Tbsp soy sauce
- 1 cup crawfish, cooked, defrosted*
- 3 Tbsp pickled ginger (optional)

Direction

- Add shrimp to a large bowl and season them with Old Bay, Seafood Seasoning, smokedpaprika, onion, and garlic powder.
- Preheat a large deep skillet with cooking oil. Add broccoli florets and stir them for a fewminutes over medium-high heat.
- Add cauliflower rice and sesame oil. Stir the mixture and cook it for two more minutes.
- Clear up the space in the middle of the skillet (push the veggie rice mixture aside, don'tremove it from the pan). Add shrimp and cook them for 2 minutes on each side.
- Mix everything up and add eggs. Scramble the eggs, adding cooked crawfish and soy sauce.
- Stir and sauté for two more minutes. Done. One-pot easy meal!

Smothered Catfish Shrimp Dinner

My recipe is easy to prepare but won't disappoint you! Tender catfish fillets are lightly breaded in a Zatarain's New Orleans Style Fish Fry mix and fried to perfection! Beautiful and crispy on the outside and light and delicious on the inside. Served with fluffy rice, smoky lemon pepper shrimp, garlic broccoli under the cheesy buttery creamy sauce! Perfection, right?!

Serving: 6

Equipment:
Rice cooker or medium pot, large bowl, large skillet or pan, spatula, 2 large flat plates or cutting
boards, deep medium microwavable bowl.

Prep time: 30 minutes
Cook time: 45 minutes
Total time: 1 hour 15 minutes

Ingredients

For the rice:
- 2 cups rice, uncooked, washed
- 4 cups water
- 1 tsp Old Bay Seasoning
- 1 tsp garlic powder
- 1 tsp Cajun seasoning, unsalted

For the fish:
- 3 catfish fillet, fresh or defrosted
- 1/2 tsp Old Bay Seasoning
- 1/2 tsp Cajun seasoning, unsalted
- 2 Tbsp yellow mustard
- 1/2 tsp garlic powder
- 1/2 tsp onion powder
- 2 large eggs
- 1 cup Zatarain's New Orleans Style Fish Fry Crispy Southern
- 2 cups cooking oil

For the shrimp:
- 1-pound large shrimp, peeled, deveined
- 2 Tbsp cooking oil
- 1 tsp Belay & Bell Seafood Seasoning
- 1 tsp MrsDash Lemon Pepper Seasoning
- 1/4 tsp onion powder

For the sauce:
- 1/2 stick of butter
- 2 tsp minced garlic*
- 1 cup heavy cream
- 1 cup Parmesan cheese, grated
- 1/4 tsp onion powder
- 1/4 tsp black pepper
- 1 tsp Hidden Valley Ranch Seasoning
- 1 tsp lemon zest
- Juice from ½ lemon

For the broccoli:
- 4 cups broccoli florets
- 1/2 tsp garlic pepper
- 1/4 tsp roasted garlic and herb seasoning

Direction

For the rice:
- Let's start with preparing the rice. Place the rice in the rice cooker or medium pot. Add water and seasonings. I highly recommend you to purchase the rice cooker as it's super easy to prepare your rice in it. Just press the setting "warm," and it's going to cook. That's it! It takes approximately 20 minutes to cook one cup of rice in the slow cooker.

For the fish:
- • Pat the catfish fillets with a paper towel to get all excess moisture out. This way batter will stick better, and the fish will be crispier!
- Lightly season fillets with Old Bay Seasoning, Cajun seasoning, mustard, garlic, and onion powder.
- Place seasoned fish into a deep large bowl, and crack the eggs into it. Using your hands, work that seasoning and eggs into each piece.
- Add Fish Fry to a large flat plate. Take catfish and gently press it down in a Fish Fry mix. Flip it over, making sure the fillet is covered with breading. Shake off any excess coating and place the catfish on a separate flat plate, wax paper, or cutting board. Repeat with the rest of the fish.
- Preheat the large skillet with cooking oil. Carefully place the fillets, making sure not to overcrowd the pan.
- Fry the fish for 5-6 minutes on each side on medium heat.
- Once they are done, set them aside on a paper towel to drain any excess oil. Repeat with the remaining fillets.

For the shrimp:
- Preheat the separate skillet with oil. Add shrimp to it and season them with Belay & Bell, MrsDash Lemon Pepper and onion powder.
- Cook shrimp for 2 minutes on each side.

For the sauce:
- Preheat the pan with butter, add garlic and heavy cream. Please bring it to a boil.
- Add Parmesan cheese, onion powder, black pepper, ranch seasoning, lemon zest, and juice. Simmer the sauce for 5-7 minutes, then add cooked shrimp.

For the broccoli:
- Place broccoli into a deep medium microwavable bowl.
- Sprinkle it with garlic pepper, garlic, and herb seasoning. Microwave the broccoli for 3-4 minutes, just until it's fork-tender.

Assemble:
- Arrange chicken on serving plates, add shrimp, rice, and broccoli on a side! Happy eating!

Note:
Minced garlic: you can mince 2 large garlic cloves or use 2 Tbsp Spice Worlds Minced Garlic
Squeeze brand.

Rasta Pasta

Meet the chicken shrimp penne of your dreams! Spicy, smoky Jamaican-styled chicken and shrimp with creamy sauce pasta. Spice up your weeknight dinner with this one-pot Rasta Pasta dish!

Serving: 4

Equipment: large bowl, pot, large skillet, wooden spatula

Prep time: 10 minutes
Cook time: 20 minutes
Total time: 30 minutes

Ingredients

For the pasta:
- One box penne pasta

For the chicken:
- 4 chicken breast, skinless, boneless
- 1 Tbsp Frank's Red Hot Honey sauce
- 2 Tbsp Jamaican Jerk Seasoning*
- 2 tsp smoked paprika
- 1 Tbsp garlic powder
- 2 Tbsp cooking oil

For the shrimp:
- 2 Tbsp cooking oil
- 1 pound shrimp, pilled, defrosted
- 1 Tbsp Jamaican Jerk Seasoning*

To assemble:
- 2 large bell peppers, sliced thin (1 red and 1 yellow)
- Pint heavy cream
- 1-2 cups Parmesan cheese

Directions

For the pasta:
- Cook one box of penne pasta, according to the package directions. Set aside.

For the chicken:
- In a large bowl, toss the chicken breast with all seasonings.
- Preheat a large skillet with cooking oil.
- Fry the chicken on medium-high for about 5 minutes on each side.
- Take it off and set it aside.

For the shrimp:
- While the pan is still hot, add more oil to it, then shrimp and spices.
- Mix with a wooden spatula and cook shrimp on medium-low 2 minutes on each side.

To assemble:
- Add bell peppers, heavy cream, and parmesan cheese to the shrimp. Stir well and cook for 2 more minutes.
- Slice cooked chicken into thin strips and add to this mixture.
- Spoon in cooked penne and stir well. Warm-up on low heat for 2 minutes, stirring.
- Divide pasta in between 4 large serving plates, sprinkle with more Parmesan cheese, and enjoy immediately!

Note:
Jamaican Jerk Seasoning: you can make your own by mixing a pinch of cayenne pepper, fine black pepper, dried thyme, brown sugar, all spice, cinnamon, cumin, garlic, and onion powder.

Creamy Seafood Lasagna

I can't wait for you to try this one-it might become a new favorite in your home! I love to cook, and I love this recipe! Its one-of-a-kind Cajun creamy taste and a delicious spin on traditional Italian lasagna flavors.

Serving: 6-8

Equipment:
9x13 inch baking dish, large pot, large bowl

Prep time: 30 minutes

Cook time: 45 minutes

Total time: 1 hour 15 minutes

Ingredients

- 1 16 oz package lasagna noodles
- 1 Tbsp salt
- 3 cups Monterey cheese

For the ricotta seafood mix:

- 1 pound shrimp, cleaned, peeled
- 2 tsp garlic pepper
- 2 tsp Cajun seasoning
- 1 tsp garlic powder
- 1 tsp onion powder
- 2 Tbsp cooking oil
- 1 pound salmon fillet, skinless, boneless
- 3 cup Ricotta cheese
- 2 eggs

For the cream sauce:

- 1/2 stick butter
- 1 Tbsp minced garlic
- 1 pint heavy cream
- 1/2 tsp garlic pepper
- 1 Tbsp garlic
- 1/2 tsp onion powder
- 3 cups shredded parmesan

Direction

For the ricotta seafood mix:

- • Season shrimp with garlic pepper, Cajun seasoning, garlic, and onion powder in a medium bowl.
- Place on preheated skillet and cook for 4 minutes on each side. Remove and set aside.
- Add more cooking oil and fry salmon fillet on the same skillet for 6-8 minutes on each side. Set aside.
- When shrimp and salmon are cooled down, chop them into bite-sized pieces. Set aside.
- In a large bowl, stir ricotta cheese with egg. Add shrimp and salmon.

For the cream sauce:

- Add butter, minced garlic, heavy cream, garlic pepper, garlic, and onion powder to the same skillet. Bring it to a boil.
- Reduce heat and add shredded parmesan cheese. Simmer for a few minutes, stirring.

For the pasta:

- Bring a large pot of salted water to a boil.
- Add pasta and cook for 8 minutes. Drain the water.

To assemble:

In a 9x13 inch baking dish, layer noodles in the following order:

1. Noodles
2. Ricotta seafood mix
3. Cream sauce
4. Shredded Monterey cheese

- Repeat layers until all ingredients are used, ensuring that there is shredded cheese on the top.
- Bake in preheated oven for 30 minutes, covered.
- Uncover and bake for another 12-15 minutes.
- Allow it to cool down for 10-15 minutes before serving.

Italian Sausage Stuffed Shells

This recipe is full of savory autumn flavors for a satisfying comfort food dinner! Jumbo shells filled with a mixture of Italian sausage, cheeses, and spices. Cooked with marinara sauce and topped with smoked Gouda, they are delicious and very juicy!

Serving: 6

Equipment: large pot, skillet, medium bowl, large baking dish

Prep time: 30 minutes

Cook time: 40 minutes

Total time: 1 hour

Ingredients

- 1 box jumbo shells
- 1 Tbsp olive oil
- 2 large spicy Italian sausages, chopped into very small pieces
- 1/2 cup ricotta cheese
- 2 cups Mozzarella cheese, shredded
- 2 tsp Tony's Cajun seasoning, unsalted
- 1 Tbsp garlic powder
- 2 tsp onion powder
- 2 tsp smoked paprika
- 1/4 tsp fine black pepper
- 1 jar marinara sauce
- 1 cup smoked Gouda cheese, shredded

Direction

- Boil the shells according to the package directions. Once they are done, rinse them under the cold water, and set them aside.
- Preheat the skillet with olive oil and add chopped sausages. Sautee them over medium high heat until they are browned and cooked, for about 4-5 minutes. Remove them from the heat.
- Mix chopped Italian sauce with ricotta cheese, shredded mozzarella cheese, and all seasonings in a medium bowl.
- Pour 1 cup of marinara into a large baking dish.
- Stuff each shell with one heaping tablespoon of filling. Place them into a baking dish over the sauce.
- Drizzle with the remaining sauce, and cover the dish with foil.
- Preheat oven to 350F and bake the shells for 40 minutes.
- Remove them from the oven, uncover them.
- Sprinkle with Gouda cheese, and bake for five more minutes, uncovered.
- Allow shells to rest for 5 minutes before serving, as they will be boiling!

Garlic & Herb Turkey Wings

It's something that makes you just want to slap the counter when eating my Garlic & Herb Turkey Wings! These oven-baked wings are baked to perfection and served with spicy potatoes
alongside green beans. Talk about a Soulful Sunday dinner!

Serving: 6-8

Equipment: 2 large bowl, large baking tray, large skillet

Prep time: 30 minutes

Cook time: 1 hour 45 minutes

Ingredients

- 4 large turkey wings, cut in half, tips removed
- 2 pounds medium red potatoes, cut in quarters
- 2 onions, chopped
- 2 cups chicken broth, reduced-sodium
- 1-2 large bell peppers, chopped
- 1 pound green beans
- 1 onion, chopped
- 2 Tbsp butter
- 2 Tbsp minced garlic*
- 1 tsp onion powder

For the wings spices:

- 1 tsp baking powder
- 1 Tbsp Cajun seasoning, unsalted
- 1 Tbsp garlic powder
- 1 Tbsp onion powder
- 1/2 tsp smoked paprika
- 2 tsp liquid smoke
- 1/2 tsp Slap Ya Mama Cajun seasoning

For the potato spices:
- 1 Tbsp parsley or chives seasoning
- 1 Tbsp Adkins Rosemary & Herb Seasoning*
- Pinch red crushed pepper
- 1 Tbsp onion powder
- 1/2 tsp salt
- 1 tsp smoked paprika
- 1 Tbsp olive oil
- 1 Tbsp MrsDash Lemon Pepper Seasoning

For the wings sauce:
- 2 Tbsp butter
- 1 tsp minced garlic
- 2 Tbsp parsley
- 1 Tbsp Old Bay seasoning, reduced salt
- 1 tsp hot sauce

Direction

- In a large bowl, add turkey wings and season them with wing spices. Set aside.
- In a separate large bowl, season the potatoes with potato spices.
- Place the seasoned potatoes on a large baking tray and add seasoned turkey wings.
- Top with onions and bell peppers.
- Gently pour chicken broth over the pan.
- Preheat oven to 375F. Bake turkey vegetable mix, covered with aluminum foil for about one hour.
- Uncover, add the heat to 450F and bake for 45 minutes more.
- While potatoes and wings are baking, prepare the green beans. Preheat a large skillet with butter. Add green beans, onion, garlic, and onion powder.
- Cover and cook on medium-low until beans are tender for about 8-10 minutes.
- Next, prepare the wing's sauce.
- Whisk the melted butter with garlic, parsley, Old Bay, and hot sauce in a small bowl.

To assemble:
- Serve wings and potatoes drizzled with wings sauce. Add green beans aside. Enjoy!

Note:
Adkins Rosemary & Herb Seasoning: you can also create your spice blend using brown sugar, fine salt, red pepper flakes, dried rosemary, oregano, basil, garlic, and onion powders. All heaping ½ tsp each.
Minced garlic: you can mince 1 garlic clove or use 2 tsp Spice Worlds Minced Garlic Squeeze brand.

Red Wine Braised Short Ribs

Soul food… with a bit of an upscale twist. Short ribs so tender, that they pull right off the bone with flavors that melt in your mouth. Once paired with these creamy mashed potatoes and the House Special Sangria, this dish is love at first bite! Let's get started.

Serving: 4 portions

Equipment:
 2 large bowls, large 5-6-quart Dutch oven, metal whisk, large pot, potato masher, large pan, 4
large serving plates.

Prep time: 30 minutes

Cook time: 2.5 hours

Total time: 3 hours

Ingredients

For the potatoes:
- 6-7 large (3.5-4 pounds) red potatoes
- 3 Tbsp garlic salt
- 6 Tbsp of butter
- 1 cup heavy cream
- 1/4 cup whole milk
- 1/4 tsp black pepper
- 1/3 cup sour cream
- Garlic salt to taste

For the short ribs:
- 12 (5.5-6 pounds) short ribs
- 1/4 cup oil for cooking
- 5-6 fresh thyme sprigs
- 3-4 fresh rosemary sprigs
- 1/4 cup white flour
- 1/2 cup dry red wine
- 3 Tbsp minced garlic*
- 1/2 cup beef broth
- 2 medium onions, roughly chopped
- 2-3 caps Worcestershire sauce
- 2-3 drops natural liquid smoke
- 2 Tbsp Adkins Rosemary & Herb Seasoning*
- 2 Tbsp Grill Masters Brown Sugar Bourbon
- 1 tsp crushed red pepper flakes

For the asparagus:
- 1 Tbsp oil for cooking
- 1 pound fresh asparagus spears
- 1 Tbsp butter
- 1/2 tsp garlic powder

To assemble:
- 1/4 cup fresh parsley, chopped

Direction

For the potatoes:
- First, wash the potatoes, and then cut them into quarters.
- Place the potatoes into a large bowl, and cover them with water. This prevents them from browning (oxidizing).

For the short ribs:
- Preheat Dutch oven on medium heat and add cooking oil.
- Gently place half of fresh thyme and rosemary sprigs into the oil. This will infuse the oil, making the ribs taste very flavorful!
- After a few minutes, remove the herbs and set them aside.
- Add short ribs and sear them for 3 minutes on each side. Take ribs out and set them aside on your cutting board. Repeat the process if needed with the remaining ribs.
- Set aside all ribs and prepare the broth for braising.
- To the remaining oil stir in the flour. Turn the heat down to low and whisk the flour with oil. Once it's thickened, add red wine and simmer for 2-3 minutes.
- Next, add minced garlic* and beef broth. Turn the heat up to medium and bring to boil.
- Once the broth is boiling, add chopped onions. Place seared ribs in a broth over the onions. Drizzle them with Worcestershire sauce and liquid smoke.
- Add Adkins Rosemary & Herb Seasoning (check out note for substitution), Grill Masters Brown Sugar Bourbon and crushed red pepper flakes.
- Gently stir the ribs, making sure that all juices and spices are mixed in.
- Top with remaining fresh thyme and rosemary sprigs.
- Preheat oven to 350 degrees Fahrenheit. Place the Dutch oven inside and cook for 3 hours, covered. Short ribs should be tender and easily pull away from the bone.

For the potatoes:
- After one hour of short ribs being in an oven, start to prepare the potatoes.
- Fill in a large pot with water and bring to boil. Add garlic, salt, and potatoes.*
- Boil the potatoes for 35-40 minutes, or until they are tender inside.
- Once the potatoes are done, drain the water and get ready for mashing.
- Add butter, heavy cream, whole milk, black pepper, and sour cream the potatoes.
- Mash with the potato masher.
- Adjust the seasoning, and add garlic salt to taste if needed. Set the mashed potatoes aside, covered.

For the asparagus:
- Prepare the asparagus. Preheat the large pan with cooking oil.
- Add asparagus and sauté it for one minute.
- Reduce heat to low; add butter and garlic powder. Cook for one minute, stirring.
- Turn off the heat and set asparagus aside.

Assemble:
- To assemble, divide mashed potatoes amongst 4 large serving plates.
- Top with juicy short ribs and asparagus.
- Drizzle with beef juices and sprinkle with fresh parsley.
- Serve and dig in!

Note:
- Minced garlic*: you can mince 6-7 large garlic cloves or use 3 Tbsp Spice Worlds Minced Garlic Squeeze brand.
- Adkins Rosemary & Herb Seasoning*: you can also create your own spice blend using brown sugar, fine salt, red pepper flakes, dried rosemary, oregano, basil, garlic, and onion powders. All heaping ½ tsp each.
- Potatoes: you can peel the potato skin off, it up to your personal likings.

Sweet & Zesty Baked Chicken

Okay, so maybe you don't feel like firing up the grill to barbecue some good chicken. No worries, I got you covered! This oven baked barbecue chicken dinner will have your house smelling like Sunday Dinner after grandma told the pastor "Take your time" for about the 3rd time! I promise it's worth the effort and the wait. Let's get started!

Serving: 4

Equipment

- 9 x 13 baking sheet
- Wire rack
- 1 large pot
- Cutting Board
- Chef's Knife
- Strainer
- Foil
- Whisk
- Ladle or large kitchen spoon

Prep time: 10 minutes
Cook time: 25 minutes
Total time: 35 minutes

Ingredients

For the spices

- Lemon pepper (Mrs. Dash Unsalted is preferred)
- Crushed Red Pepper
- Garlic powder
- Onion Powder
- Black Pepper
- Smoked Paprika
- Parsley
- Garlic Salt
- Chicken Bouillon
- Cajun Seasoning
- Hickory liquid smoke
- Honey

- Brown Sugar
- Worcestershire sauce

For the cabbage:
- 1 head of Cabbage
- 1/2 slab of bacon cut into small pieces
- ½ white or yellow onion roughly chopped

For the chicken:
- 4-6 Chicken Thighs or Leg Quarters (your choice of skinless or skin on)
- Baking Powder
- 1 cup of your favorite BBQ sauce

For the mac & cheese:
- 12-16 oz large elbow noodles
- ¼ cup all-purpose flour
- ½ stick of unsalted butter
- 4 oz whipped cream cheese
- 1 pint of Heavy Whipping Cream
- 2% milk
- 4 oz. sour cream
- ½ block of sharp cheddar cheese
- ½ block of Colby jack cheese
- 1/2 block of gouda or parmesan cheese or gouda

Directions

- Preheat oven to 400 degrees F, pat cleaned chicken dry with a paper towel.
- Season chicken with 1-1.5 tsp of Cajun seasoning, smoked paprika, garlic powder, unsalted lemon pepper, and baking powder. (Mix ingredients into chicken and ensure to get seasoning under the skin as well).
- Cook chicken at 400 degrees for 1 hour.
- Finely chop and wash cabbage thoroughly, then set aside in a bowl for future use.
- Boil pasta noodles on high for 7-8 minutes or until al dente. (Pro tip: add one chicken bouillon cube to water).
- Grate all cheeses and set them aside while noodles are boiling.
- Add ½ stick butter into a large pot and melt on medium heat. Add in ¼ cup flour once the butter has melted, then whisk ingredients together to complete roux. (Roux should be a light-yellow color still).
- Add 1 pint of heavy whipping cream to your pot, and then bring to a light boil. Once heavy cream comes to a boil, add in half of your grated cheese. Reduce heat to low and add in ¼ cup sour cream, 4 oz whipped cream cheese, Cajun seasoning to taste, garlic powder, and smoked paprika.
- Once ingredients are incorporated, add 1-2 cups of milk into your cheese sauce. Remove cheese sauce from heat and add in pasta noodles. Stir pasta into cheese sauce until all noodles are covered.
- Layer macaroni into a baking dish or large cast-iron skillet in the following steps. Pour in half of the macaroni, add in a handful of grated cheese, more macaroni, top off with grated cheese. Once complete, sprinkle parsley and paprika over macaroni.
- Bake macaroni at 400 degrees for 20-25 mins.
- Cook bacon on medium-high heat in a large pot or deep skillet for 5 minutes
- Add in roughly chopped onion and allow to cook for 4 minutes
- Add cabbage to the pot, season with 1 tbsp. of each (garlic powder, onion powder, liquid smoke, crushed red pepper, liquid smoke, and garlic salt); cover with a lid and allow to cook for 18-20 minutes. Lift lid and stir cabbage greens around halfway through cooking. Remove from heat
- Once chicken is done cooking, brush barbecue sauce over chicken to evenly coat.
- Plate and Enjoy

Parmesan Crusted Tuscan Chicken

Bring yourself to the green fields of Tuscany with this Parmesan Crusted Tuscan Chicken recipe.

It looks as good as it tastes! The flavors come together so well, and you will love the way the Italian herbs, cheese, spinach, creamy sauce pair with juicy chicken, garlicky roasted potatoes, and earthy asparagus.

Enjoy this fuss-free delicious meal any day of the week!

Serving: 4

Equipment

large bowl, cooking pan for oven, large skillet, medium deep pot.

Prep time: 20 minutes

Cook time: 40 minutes

Total time: 1 hour

Ingredients

For the chicken:
- 2 large chicken breasts, boneless, skinless
- 1 Tbsp cooking oil
- 1 Tbsp Tuscan seasoning*
- 2 Tbsp Hidden Valley Ranch Seasoning
- 2 tsp minced onion seasoning
- 1 tsp MrsDash Lemon Pepper Seasoning
- 3 eggs

For the potatoes:
- 1 pound baby potatoes, cut in halves
- 2 Tbsp cooking oil, refined
- 1 Tbsp garlic salt
- 1 Tbsp garlic powder
- 2 tsp onion powder
- 1 tsp black pepper

For the bread crumbs mix:
- 1 cup Parmesan & Romano cheese, gated
- 1 cup Panko bread crumbs
- 1 Tbsp Tuscan seasoning
- 2 Tbsp Hidden Valley Ranch Seasoning
- 2 tsp minced onion seasoning
- 2 tsp MrsDash Lemon Pepper Seasoning

For the Tuscan Sauce:
- 1 pound fresh baby spinach
- 1-pint heavy whipping cream
- 2 tsp minced garlic
- 2 Tbsp Hidden Valley Ranch Seasoning
- 1 cup Mozzarella cheese, shredded
- 2 tsp Tuscan seasoning
- Pinch garlic salt
- Pinch crushed red pepper flakes
- 1/4 cup Parmesan & Romano cheese, gated
- 1/2 cup sun-dried tomatoes, chopped

For the asparagus:
- 1 pound fresh asparagus

Direction

For the chicken:
- Prepare the chicken: make a slit horizontally, dividing the breast in half and stopping ½ inch from the opposite side. When it's done, open up the chicken like a "book."
- Repeat with all chicken.
- Next, rub each breast with Tuscan seasoning, Valley Ranch, minced onion, and MrsDash.
- Allow them to rest while preparing the potatoes.

For the potatoes:
- In a large bowl, toss the potatoes with oil, salt, black pepper, garlic, and onion powder.
- Preheat the oven to 425F and roast them for 30 minutes. For the chicken (continue):
- Prepare the egg wash: crack the eggs into a bowl and whisk them with a fork. Set aside.

For the bread crumbs mix:
- In a large bowl, stir all ingredients for the mix. For the chicken (continue):
- Bread the chicken: take the breast and dip it into the egg wash.
- Repeat with the remaining chicken.
- Preheat the skillet with cooking oil on medium heat.
- Carefully place the chicken into the skillet, and cook for 5-6 minutes on each side.
- Place cooked chicken on a paper towel to drain any excess grease.

For the Tuscan Sauce:
- Preheat medium pot with heavy cream.
- Add the rest of the ingredients for the sauce, and bring it to a boil.
- Reduce the heat, stir and simmer the sauce for 10 minutes on low heat, uncovered.

For the asparagus:
- Place it into a microwavable bowl, or buy already ready to steam in bag asparagus.
- Microwave it for a few minutes.

To assemble:
- Place chicken breast on a serving plate with a side of potatoes and asparagus. Drizzle with creamy Tuscan sauce and enjoy!

Note

Tuscan seasoning: you can easily make your own by mixing a pinch of Italian herbs, smoked paprika, lemon zest, garlic, and onion powder.

Minced garlic: you can mince 2 large garlic cloves or use 2 Tbsp Spice Worlds Minced Garlic Squeeze brand.

Loaded Seafood Baked Potatoes

If you are having a great day, look forward to it getting even better!
Let me introduce you to these loaded crispy baked potatoes stuffed with creamy Cajun sauce,
battery smoky lobster meat, shrimp, and crab meat. This recipe is a great side dish or a meal itself. Smooth cheesy, decadent, deliciously ultimate THE best Loaded Seafood Baked Potatoes!

Serving: 8

Equipment: baking sheet, large bowl, large skillet, kitchen shears

Prep time: 30 minutes

Cook time: 1 hour

Total time: 1 hour and 30 minutes

Ingredients

For the potatoes:
- 8 large potatoes
- Cooking spray
- 1/2 tsp Old Bay Seasoning Garlic & Herbs
- 1/4 tsp fine black pepper

For the lobster tails:
- 4 lobster tails
- 1/4 tsp Old Bay Seasoning Garlic & Herbs
- Pinch Blackened Old Bay Seasoning
- Pinch smoked paprika
- Pinch fine black pepper
- 1/2 tsp Cajun seasoning, unsalted

For the shrimp:
- 2 pounds large shrimp, peeled, cleaned
- 1 tsp Old Bay Seasoning Garlic & Herbs
- 1/4 tsp Blackened Old Bay Seasoning
- 1/2 tsp smoked paprika
- ½ tsp fine black pepper
- 1/2 tsp Cajun seasoning, unsalted

For the sauce:
- 1/2 stick butter, unsalted
- 2 tsp white flour
- 1/2 small onion, chopped
- 2 Tbsp minced garlic*
- 2 medium bell peppers, sliced
- Pint heavy cream
- 4 oz. whipped cream cheese
- 1/4 tsp Old Bay Seasoning Garlic & Herbs
- Pinch fine black pepper
- 1 tsp Cajun seasoning, unsalted
- 1/4 tsp smoked paprika

- 1 cup cooked crab meat
- 1 cup your favorite shredded cheese

Direction

For the potatoes:

- Place potatoes on a baking sheet. Using the fork, poke 6-8 whole thought the skin of the potatoes. This will help them to steam better inside.
- Preheat oven to 400F.
- Bake the potatoes for about 45 minutes, uncovered.
- Carefully remove them from the oven and spray the potatoes with cooking spray.
- Sprinkle them with Old Bay and black pepper.
- Place them back into the oven for another 20 minutes, uncovered.

For the lobster tails:

- While potatoes have been cooking last 20 minutes, start preparing the seafood mixture.
- Thaw out lobster tails if frozen. Then you want to crack your lobster tail open.
- Take the kitchen shears, and cut along the top of the shell, just a little underneath. Cut it back of the tail.
- Run your fingers underneath the lobster tail between the meat and the shell to loosen it. Remove all dirt, veins, and rinse with water if needed.
- Using your fingers, gently open up the shell and pop the meat out of the shell. Repeat with the rest of the lobster tails.
- Next, cut them into bite-size pieces and place into a large bowl.
- Season them with Old Bay seasonings, smoked paprika, black pepper, and Cajun seasoning.
- Preheat large skillet with a cooking spray.
- Cook lobsters tails for about 2 minutes on each side over medium heat.
- Remove lobster tails from the skillet. Set aside.

For the shrimp:

- For the shrimp, use the same skillet and pre-season them before cooking.
- Cook shrimp for 2 minutes on each side over medium heat.
- Remove them from the skillet. Set aside.

For the sauce:

- Add butter to the skillet and let it melt down over low heat.
- Sprinkle melted butter with white flour. Stir it on low heat for one minute.
- Next, add chopped onion, minced garlic, and sliced bell peppers. Cook them for 2-3 minutes, stirring.
- Season with Old Bay, fine black pepper, Cajun seasoning, and smoked paprika. Lower the heat to a very low and simmer for 2 more minutes.

To finish:

- Add shrimp, lobsters, and cooked crab meat (or crawfish) to the sauce. Sprinkle with your favorite shredded cheese. Stir well. Turn off the heat and remove the pan from the heat.
- Remove the potatoes from the oven, and allow them to rest on a serving plate for 10 minutes before slicing them open.
- Slice each potato lengthwise and open them up very carefully as they can be still very hot!
- Generously spoon the seafood sauce in the middle of each potato and top it over.
- Garnish with fresh scallions (optional).
- Enjoy!

Note:

Minced garlic: you can mince 2 garlic cloves or use 2 Tbsp. Spice Worlds Minced Garlic Squeeze brand.

Crabmeat: to reduce the cost of this meal, replace it with cooked, cleaned crawfish.

Tequila Lime Chicken

Somehow, I snuck in a couple of healthier options for when the holiday season is over, and you're trying to get your life back together. This tequila lime chicken dinner is also good year round as a great meal prep option. This recipe is not one that you want to sleep on or pass over. Let's get started!

Serving: 4

Equipment:
 Rice cooker or medium pot, large bowl, large cast iron skillet, long lighter, tongs.

Prep time: 10 minutes

Cook time: 1 hour

Total time: 1 hour minutes

Ingredients

For the rice:
- 1-2 cups brown or Jasmine rice, uncooked, washed
- 2-4 cups water
- 2 Tbsp Tomato Bouillon
- 2 tsp tomato paste

For the chicken:
- 2 chicken breasts, medium-sized, skinless, boneless (butterflied into 4 halves)
- 1 Tbsp onion powder
- 1 Tbsp Garlic Salt* (or to taste level)
- 1 Tbsp garlic powder
- 1 Tbsp store-bought cilantro paste*
- 1 lime, juiced
- 2 tsp minced garlic*
- 1.5 tbs. Grapeseed Oil
- 1/4 cup Casamigos Tequila (optional)

For the broccoli:
- 2 pounds broccoli, washed
- 1 Tbsp lemon pepper
- 2 Tbsp cooking oil

Direction

For the rice:

- Let's start with preparing the rice. Place the rice in the rice cooker or medium pot. Add water and tomato bouillon. I highly recommend you purchase the rice cooker as it's super easy to prepare your rice in it. Just press the setting "warm," and it's going to cook. That's it! It takes approximately 25 minutes to cook two cups of rice in the slow cooker.
- If no rice cooker, wash the rice to clear off some of the starch. Bring water, tomato bouillon, and tomato paste to a boil then add in rice (2 cups of water per 1 cup of rice). Reduce heat to the lowest setting, then cover with a lid to cook for 18-20 mins. Remove pot from the burner while keeping the lid on, then allow steam to finish cooking rice for another 5 minutes. Remove lid and fluff rice with a fork.
- Place chicken in a large bowl and season it with onion powder, garlic salt, garlic powder, cilantro paste, lime juice, and garlic. Massage the chicken to incorporate all flavors.
- Allow it to marinate for at least 30 minutes to 24 hours, covered, and refrigerated. (24 hours gets best flavor)
- Preheat cast-iron skillet with Grapeseed Oil on medium-to-medium high heat.
- Once oil has gotten hot (appx. 3 mins), grab the tequila and pour it on a pan carefully. The alcohol will cook out as the chicken cooks.
- Add chicken and cook it on medium heat for 5 minutes. If you like even more flavors, flip it add an extra lime juice and minced garlic (juice from one more lime, and 1-2 Tbsp of minced garlic). Cook for 5 more minutes.

For the broccoli:

- Preheat oven to 450F.
- Toss washed broccoli with lemon pepper and oil.
- Cook it for 7-10 minutes.

To assemble:

- Serve chicken with rice, broccoli, topped with leftover sauce from the pan. Store-bought cilantro paste*: to substitute, add 1 cup of cilantro with 3 Tbsp of oil in a small blender, puree for 30 seconds. Season with salt to taste.
- **Minced garlic**: you can mince 1 garlic clove or use 2 tsp Spice Worlds Minced Garlic Squeeze brand.

Honey Lime Jalapeno Chicken

These perfectly seasoned chicken breasts are paired with smoky garlicky sweet potatoes and nutritious kale greens. It's topped with sweet-spicy citrusy sauce. Packed with flavors and vitamins, this recipe is healthy, tasty, and done in no time!

Serving: 4

Equipment:

Large bowl, large baking pan, aluminum foil, large pot, cast iron skillet, spatula, small bowl, 4 serving plates.

Prep time: 20 minutes

Cook time: 20 minutes

Total time: 40 minutes

Ingredients

For the potatoes:
- 4-5 large sweet potatoes
- 1/4 tsp fine sea salt
- 1 tsp Kinder's Rub, Brown Sugar*
- 1 tsp roasted garlic seasoning
- 1/4 tsp black pepper
- 2 tsp smoked paprika
- 2 Tsp cooking oil

For the kale:
- 32 oz vegetable stock
- 3 Tsp olive oil
- 1 medium to large onion, diced
- 1 red bell pepper, sliced
- 2 small tomatoes, diced
- 2 pounds fresh kale greens
- 4 minced garlic cloves*
- 1 Tbsp MrsDash unsalted seasoning
- 1/4 tsp fine sea salt

For the chicken:
- 4 medium-sized chicken breast, skin & bone removed
- 1/4 tsp fine sea salt
- 1 tsp Kinder's Rub, Brown Sugar*
- 1 tsp roasted garlic seasoning
- ¼ tsp black pepper
- 1 Tsp smoked paprika
- 2 Tbsp cooking oil

For the honey Jalapeno sauce:
- 1/2 cup honey
- 2 jalapeno peppers, diced
- 2-3 garlic cloves, minced*
- 1 large fresh lime

Direction

For the potatoes:
- Slice the potatoes into chunks, leaving the skin on.
- Next, add them to a large bowl, and season with fine sea salt, Kinder's Rub, roasted garlic seasoning, black pepper, and smoked paprika.
- Toss the potatoes well to incorporate the flavors.
- Line a baking sheet with aluminum foil. Spread the potatoes in one even layer and drizzle them with oil.
- Bake the potatoes at 450F for about 35-40 minutes, stirring once.

For the kale:
- Pour vegetable stock into a large pot, and bring it to a boil.
- Add kale green greens.
- Simmer them for 3-5 minutes.
- Preheat the skillet with olive oil and add onion, bell peppers, and tomatoes. Sauté the vegetables on high-medium heat up to 3 minutes.
- Next, mix in kale, garlic, MrsDash seasoning, and salt. Stir everything and cook on medium heat for 4 more minutes.

For the chicken:
- First, preheat cast skillet with oil.
- Place chicken into a large bowl, and rub with all spices.
- Next, transfer it to a hot skillet.
- Cook the chicken on medium-high heat for 5 minutes on each side. Once done, remove it from the skillet, and set aside.

For the honey Jalapeno sauce:
- Preheat the skillet on medium-low.
- Pour honey and sprinkle with diced jalapeno pepper.
- Bring it to a light simmer.
- Drizzle the sauce with lime juice, and minced garlic.
- Continue to simmer it on low heat for 10 minutes. Don't forget to stir a few times.
- Remove the sauce from the skillet, and pour into a bowl. Set aside.

To assemble:
- Arrange cooked chicken on a serving plate and generously drizzle it the honey jalapeno sauce over. Place kale greens on a side and potatoes.

Note:
• **Kinder's Rub, Brown Sugar**: you replace this with equal amounts (1/4 tsp each): red chili pepper flakes, garlic powder, and brown sugar.
• **Minced garlic**: you can mince 4 large garlic cloves or use 2 Tbsp Spice Worlds Minced Garlic Squeeze brand.

Sticky-Icky Bourbon Candied Yams

Bourbon Spiked Candied Yams are a must-have on every holiday dinner table! This recipe is a classic holiday feast spiked with this irresistible bourbon brown sugar sauce that'll have you licking the spoon and bowl clean.

Serving: 6-8

Equipment
small pot, large bowl, 9x13 inches baking pan

Prep time: 20 minutes

Cook time: 50 minutes

Total time: 1 hour 10 minutes

Ingredients

- 3 pounds yams or sweet potatoes, peeled, diced into small cubes
- 1 stick butter, unsalted
- 1 cup brown sugar
- 1 tbsp cinnamon
- 1 tsp nutmeg
- 1/3 cup maple syrup
- ¼ - ½ cup Jack Daniel's Honey or Maple
- 1 tsp lemon juice

Direction

- To a small pot, add cubed butter and stir in until melted over low heat.
- Mix in brown sugar, cinnamon, nutmeg, maple syrup, lemon juice and bourbon.
- Add potatoes to a large bowl and pour this mixture over them. Toss the potatoes, making sure they are all coated.
- Preheat oven to 350F.
- Place the potatoes into a baking dish. Pour any leftover sweet sauce from the bowl over them.
- Bake the potatoes covered for 40 minutes, stirring twice.
- Add heat to 400F and bake them for ten to twenty more minutes. Yams should be fork tender, but not falling apart.
- Serve and enjoy!

Soulful & Southern Collard Greens

Collard greens cooked with the soul of somebody's grandma that has the baby fat on the back of their arm. Full of flavor and LOVE! Let's get started!

Serving: 10-12

Equipment
two large cooking pots

Prep time: 30 minutes

Cook time: 2 hours

Total time: 2.5 hours

Ingredients

For the greens:
- 6 bunches fresh collard greens
- 1 Tbsp salt
- 2 tsp garlic powder
- 2 tsp onion powder
- 2 Tbsp sugar
- 1 tsp crushed red pepper
- 2 Tbsp Cajun seasoning (or to taste)
- 1 tbsp apple cider vinegar
- 1/4 cup cooking oil
- 3 cups reduced sodium chicken broth

For the neck bones:
- 3 pounds neck bones

Direction

For the greens:
- Prepare the collard greens: remove the thick stems out.
- Fill the kitchen sink with water and toss the greens up and down to loosen any sand and dirt. Change the water at least three times and rinse the collard green until you don't see any dirt and the water is clean.
- Stack about 6-8 leaves on top of each other, roll up like a cigar, and cut into ½-inch ribbons. Repeat with remaining leaves.
- Place greens in a large pot and add the rest of the ingredients above.
- Boil greens for 2 hours on medium heat, covered. Stir every 10-15 minutes. My tip: set the timer! Add in neckbones to boil simultaneously with greens
- Enjoy!

Gourmet Lobster Mac and Cheese

This mac and cheese recipe is one that will gain you bragging rights and well-deserved respect. One thing for sure, the mac is MAC'NG in this recipe. (That's not a real word, but it'll make sense after your first couple of bites.)

Serving: 6-8

Equipment: large skillet, kitchen shears, whisk, wooden spoon, large pot, deep glass baking dish

Prep time: 15 minutes

Cook time: 30 minutes

Total time: 45 minutes

Ingredients

For the pasta:
- 1 box macaroni pasta

For the lobster tails:
- 6 large lobster tails
- Cooking spray

For the roux:
- 1/2 stick butter
- 1/4 cup white flour
- Pint heavy cream
- ½ block of each; smoked Gouda and Parmesan cheese (grate the cheeses)
- 4 oz. whipped cream cheese
- 1/2 cup full-fat sour cream
- 1 cup full-fat milk
- 1 cup chicken broth
- 1 Tbsp smoked paprika
- 1 Tbsp garlic powder
- Tony Creole seasoning to taste
- 2 Tbsps Cajun seasoning, unsalted

To assemble:
- 1 cup of each cheese, shredded
- 1/4 tsp paprika

Direction

For the pasta:
- Bring a large pot with water to a boil. Add macaroni and cook for about 7 minutes.
- Drain them and set them aside.

For the lobster tails:
- Thaw out lobster tails if frozen. Then you want to crack your lobster tail open.
- Take the kitchen shears, and cut along the top of the shell, just a little underneath. Cut it to the back of the tail.
- Run your fingers underneath the lobster tail between the meat and the shell to loosen it. Remove all dirt, veins, and rinse with water if needed.
- Using your fingers, gently open up the shell and pop the meat out of the shell. Repeat with the rest of the lobster tail.
- Preheat large skillet with a cooking spray.
- Cook lobsters tails for about 2 minutes on each side over medium heat.
- Remove lobster tails from the skillet, and cut them into bite-size pieces. Set aside.

For the roux:
- In a large pot, melt butter over the low heat.
- Add white flour then heavy cream. Whisk and bring it to a boil.
- Then add 1/3 of your grated cheese, whipped cream cheese, sour cream, full-fat milk, and chicken broth. Stir and continue cooking for a few more minutes over low heat.
- Next, build its spices. Sprinkle the roux with smoked paprika, garlic powder, Tony seasoning, and Cajun seasoning. Stir well.
- Add cooked macaroni and chopped lobster tails. Gently stir.

To assemble:
- Transfer ½ macaroni mixture into a deep glass baking pan. Sprinkle pasta with 1/3 of cheese and cover it with the rest of the mac.
- Top with more cheese and sprinkle with paprika.
- Preheat oven to 400 F
- Bake lobster mac for 20-30 minutes, uncovered. The top will be nice and golden brown.
- Allow macaroni to cool for 10-15 minutes before serving
- Serve and enjoy this gourmet recipe!

Cheesy Au Gratin Potatoes

The ideal dish to add to your upcoming holiday menus! This classic and comforting recipe with my twist: Cajun bell pepper cheesy sauce! Enjoy my simple recipe made from scratch!

Serving: 8

Equipment: medium skillet, 9x13 baking casserole dish lined with parchment paper, aluminum foil

Prep time: 15 minutes

Cook time: 1 hour

Total time: 1 and 15 minutes

Ingredients

- 2 Tbsp olive oil
- 3 large bell peppers, cleaned, sliced thin
- 1 medium onion, sliced thin
- 3 pounds white potatoes, sliced thick about 1/8 inch
- 2 cups smoked Gouda cheese, shredded
- 3 cups Gruyere cheese, shredded

For the sauce:

- 1/4 cup butter, cubed
- 3 Tbsp minced garlic
- 2 Tbsp white flour
- 3 tsp Creole Seasoning, salted
- 1 tsp onion powder
- 1/4 tsp fine black pepper
- Pinch nutmeg
- 1 cup chicken broth
- 1 cup heavy cream

Direction

- Preheat a large skillet with olive oil over medium heat.
- Add sliced bell peppers and onion, and fry them for 5 minutes, stirring. Remove them from the heat, and set them aside.

For the sauce:
- In a medium skillet, add butter and melt it over low heat. Sprinkle it with minced garlic and sauté it for one minute.
- Add in the flour, creole seasoning, onion powder, black pepper, nutmeg, and stir for one more minute.
- Pour in the broth and heavy cream. Whisk. Cook for 5 more minutes, whisking.

For the potatoes:
- Spread half of the sliced potatoes on the bottom of the baking dish.
- Top them with bell pepper onion mix.
- Sprinkle with shredded Gouda cheese.
- Top with remaining sliced potatoes.
- Sprinkle them with shredded Gruyere cheese.
- Gently pour the sauce over.
- Preheat oven to 400F.
- Bake the potatoes covered with aluminum foil for 45 minutes.
- Very carefully remove the foil and bake them uncovered for another 25-30 minutes, until the top is browned and potatoes are cooked through.

Honey Baked Ham

I'm willing to bet that you're on this recipe because of several failed attempts at eating dry turkey (not mine, but you get what I'm saying.) From the sticky-icky glaze to the tenderness of the ham… you and your family will DEVOUR this honey baked ham. Let's get it!

Serving: 6-8

Equipment:
Large roasting pan, heavy duty aluminum foil, medium bowl

Prep time: 10 minutes

Cook time: 15 minutes per pound

One hour and 30 minutes total

Ingredients

- One 6-pound bone-in spiral-cut cooked ham
- Toothpicks
- 1 small can of pineapple rings

For the glaze:
- 1/4 cup brown sugar
- 3/4 white sugar
- 1 cup pineapple juice

- 1/2 cup honey
- ¼ tsp cinnamon
- ¼ tsp nutmeg
- ¼ tsp fine black pepper
- 2 Tbsp thyme seasoning
- 2 Tbsp rosemary seasoning

Direction

- Lay the ham on the large roasting pan. Then cover it with heavy-duty aluminum foil.
- Preheat oven to 325F.
- Decorate the ham with pineapple rings using toothpicks to hold the pineapples in place.
- Prepare the glaze: Whisk together all ingredients in a medium bowl.
- Transfer them into a medium pot and bring it to a simmer. Continue simmering and stirring for about 1.5-2 minutes.
- Turn off the heat and remove the pot from the heat.
- Pour 1/3 of glaze over your ham. Be sure to get glaze in between all crevices. When the oven is ready, cover your ham with aluminum foil, and bake it for 15 minutes per pound: one hour and 30 minutes total.
- When the ham is about to be done (approximately 10-15 minutes prior), take it out of the oven. Be careful removing the aluminum foil off!
- Pour 1/3 of the glaze over the ham. Please put it back into the oven, uncovered.
- Increase oven temperature to 400F and bake the ham for 10-15 minutes.
- Remove the ham from the oven and brush it with leftover glaze.
- Loosely cover with aluminum foil. Let it rest for 15 more minutes before carving.

Seafood Cornbread Dressing

Other than making sure the mac and cheese is on point, this is top 3 MOST IMPORTANT dishes to not mess up at Thanksgiving Dinner.

Serving: 6-8
Equipment: large bowl, whisk, greased 9 x 13 casserole dish, skillet
Prep time: 50 minutes
Cook time: 35 minutes
Total time: 1 hour 25 minutes

Ingredients

- 2 Tbsp butter
- 3 garlic cloves, minced
- 1 pound shrimp peeled, cleaned, chopped into bite-sized pieces
- 1 pound lump crab meat

For the cornbread:
- 3 large eggs
- 1 cup whole milk
- Three 8-ounce boxes of Jiffy Corn Muffin Mix

For the dressing:

- ¼ cup butter, cubed
- 1 cup onion, diced
- 1 cup green bell peppers, diced
- 1 cup celery, diced
- 4 cups chicken or seafood broth
- 1 (10.75 oz) can of Campbell's Cream of Chicken
- 2 large eggs
- Poultry Seasoning to taste
- 2 tsp. Sage
- 1 Tbsp Tony's Creole seasoning, unsalted
- Cajun Seasoning of choice to taste
- 1 Tbsp garlic powder
- 1 Tbsp. black pepper
- 2 tsp onion powder
- 2 tsp smoked paprika

Direction

- Prepare the cornbread first— preheat the oven to 400F.
- In a large bowl, whisk eggs with milk. Then add Jiffy Corn Muffin Mix.
- Pour this into the 8 x 8 baking dish and bake for 20-30 minutes or until the top is nicely golden brown. (You should be able to stick a toothpick through to the bottom, and it come out clean.)
- Remove the cornbread from the oven, allow it to cool down.
- While the cornbread is cooling down, prepare the dressing.
- Preheat the skillet with butter and minced garlic. Add chopped shrimp and crab. Cook them for 4 minutes, stirring. Remove the seafood mix from the skillet and set them aside.
- Preheat the large deep pot with butter. Add onions, bell peppers, and celery, then sauté them for 3 minutes over medium high heat, stirring. Remove it from the stove.
- Add cooked shrimp, crabmeat, and the rest of the ingredients for the dressing.
- Crumble cooled cornbread into the mixture. Stir everything well.
- Preheat oven to 350 degrees
- Pour the dressing into a greased 9 x 13 casserole dish.
- Bake it for 35-45 minutes or until the dressing is golden brown.

Air Fried Cornish Hens Two Ways

1) Rosemary Thyme

2) Smoky Cajun

Air-fried Cornish hens with crispy skin and juicy meat are the best for upcoming Thanksgiving dinner!
Prepare them with rosemary and thyme traditional autumn flavors, or try something new:
Smoky Cajun.
Or make both recipes and surprise your family and friends! They are not hard to prepare, but delicious, flavorful

Equipment
Small blender, large air fryer
Prep time: 40 minutes
Cook time: 50 minutes
Total time: 1 hour 30 minutes

Ingredients

For the Rosemary Thyme Marinade:
- 1 spring of fresh rosemary
- 1 spring of fresh thyme
- 2 Tbsp minced garlic*
- 3/4 cup cooking oil
- 1 Tbs seasoned salt*
- 1 tsp fine black pepper

For the Rosemary Thyme Hens:
- 2 medium Cornish hens, goblets removed, defrosted, washed
- 4 tsp minced garlic*
- 4 springs of fresh thyme
- 4 thick lemon wedges
- 1 tsp seasoned salt*
- 1 tsp garlic powder

For the Cajun hens:
- 2 medium Cornish hens, goblets removed, defrosted, washed
- 1 bottle Tony Ingestible Marinade
- 1 tsp Tony Creole seasoning
- 1/2 tsp Blackened Old Bay Seasoning

Direction

For the Rosemary Thyme Marinade:
- First, remove leaves off the rosemary and thyme springs.
- Then add them to a small blender.
- Pour cooking oil over the herbs, add minced garlic, seasoned salt, and fine black pepper.
- Blend well and set aside.

To assemble the Rosemary Thyme Hens:
- Place Cornish hens on cutting boards and pat them dry with a paper towel. This will ensure their skin will become crispier during the cooking process.
- Place inside each hen's cavity: 2 tsp minced garlic, 2 springs of fresh thyme, 2 lemon wedges, seasoned salt, and garlic powder.
- Season the hens on both sides with seasoned salt and garlic powder.
- Massage them with the marinade, making sure everything is covered.

For the Cajun hens:
- Assemble the injector that comes with the marinade.
- Inject the hens all around the breast, thighs. Use one injector for one hen.
- Next, run the skins of the hens with Tony and Old Bay Seasoning.

To air-fry both types of hens:
- Preheat air fryer to 400F
- Place hens into the air-fryer buckets and cook them for 50 minutes.
- Flip halfway through.
- Remove the hens, let them rest on a cutting board for 10 minutes before serving. Happy Thanksgiving!

Note:
Minced garlic: you can mince 1 garlic cloves or use 2 tsp Spice Worlds Minced Garlic Squeeze brand.
Seasoned salt: if you don't have it, use an equal amount of each (pinch): fine salt, fine black pepper, garlic and onion powder, red pepper flakes.

Henny-Nog

I know the Christmas holiday song across America is "All I want for Christmas", but THIS drink has more of a "In my mind" from The Temptations' "Silent Night" feel to it. Call off from work tomorrow and enjoy one or three of these! Let's get it!

Serving: 2
Equipment:
small pot, tablespoon, 2 bowls, electric mixer

Prep time: 10-12 minutes

Cook time: 10 minutes

Total time: 20 minutes

Ingredients

- 2 very fresh eggs
- ¼ cup brown sugar
- 1/2 cup whole milk
- 1/4 cup heavy cream
- 1/4 tsp vanilla extract
- Pinch nutmeg
- 1 shot Bumbu rum
- 1 shot Hennessey
- Pinch cinnamon
- 2 tsp powdered sugar

Direction

- First, separate the egg whites from the egg yolks.
- Then in a small bowl, whisk the yolks with brown sugar.
- Preheat a small pot with milk and heavy cream over low heat, stirring. When it starts to bubble, remove the milk from the stove.
- Using a tablespoon, add hot milk, one tablespoon at a time, into whisked brown sugar yolk mixture. Stir in vanilla extract, nutmeg, cinnamon, Hennessey, and rum. Set aside.
- In a separate bowl, using the electric mixer, beat egg whites with powdered sugar until a ribbon-like texture begins to form.
- Gently pour the eggs whites into the eggnog. Fold the mixture.
- Divide the eggnog in between two serving glasses and enjoy it!

Cajun Fried Turkey

Make last year the LAST year of eating dry turkey. This Cajun fried turkey will change life for you and your family. If you're cooking this turkey for the in-laws, I can promise you that they'll love you and ask for this dish over and over! Let's get started.

Safety tips:
1. To have critical safety equipment such as fryer pot specific for a turkey fryer, propane tank, work heavy duty grilling gloves, Class B fire extinguisher (for chemical fires) and the thermometer.
2. Pick the proper place. Never fry a turkey indoors or inside the garage! It must be outside, making sure you are at least 10 feet away from the building or anything that can be caught on fire!
3. Never fry the turkey in the rain or during the strong winds, creating fire hazards.
4. Make sure the frying place is away from running pets and kids!
5. Wear closed-toe shoes to avoid any hot oil drippings
6. The amount of oil will depend on the size of the turkey and fryer basket.

Generally, you will need 3 gallons of oil for a 30 qt. pot and 3 1/3 gallons of oil for a 32 qt. pot. You can determine the proper amount of oil before cooking: add the turkey into the pot you will be frying it and pour water over until the turkey is 5-6 inches below the top of the pot. This will be the amount of oil you will need.

Equipment

Fryer pot specific for a turkey fryer, propane tank, work gloves, Class B fire extinguisher, thermometer and probe thermometer

Prep time: 2 days

Cook time: 30-35 minutes

Ingredients

- 13-14 pound turkey, thoroughly defrosted, giblets removed, patted dry
- About 4 gallons of peanut oil
- Dry brine for the 15-pound turkey:
- 2 Tbsp coarse sea salt
- 2 Tbsp Cajun seasoning
- 1 Tbsp smoked paprika
- 1 Tbsp brown sugar
- 1 tsp garlic powder
- 1 tsp onion powder
- 4 garlic cloves, minced

Direction

- In a small bowl, mix all ingredients for the dry brine.
- Use your finger to loosen up the skin from the turkey breast and legs. Rub with spices in between the skin and meat. Season the whole turkey, including the cavity.
- Lay the turkey-side up in a deep pan and cover. Refrigerate for two days.
- Remove the turkey one hour before frying, let it air dry a room temperature for 1 hour before cooking. Remove all excess moisture with a paper towel.
- Add peanut oil to a 30-quart pot and set it over high heat on an outside propane burner with a sturdy structure! Bring the temperature to 250F, then slowly lower the turkey into the oil.
- Let it cook for a few minutes, and once the temperature reaches 350F, lower the heat and maintain this 350F during cooking.
- Fry for 30 minutes and check the temperature of the turkey breast with a probe thermometer. When the breast temperature reaches 151F, gently remove the turkey from the oil. Allow turkey to rest for 30-35 minutes before carving!

Sweet Potato Cheesecake

I'll just let the title speak for itself here. Two of the greatest desserts combined into one AMAZING dish.

Serving: 8-12

Equipment: large bowl, hand blender, medium bowl, potato masher

Prep time: 1 hour

Cook time: 40-45 minutes

Total time: 1 hour 45 minutes

Ingredients

- 8 oz cream cheese (bring to room temp)
- 1/2 cup white sugar
- 1/2 cup brown sugar
- 2 medium sized sweet potatoes, boiled, cooled down
- 1/2 tsp nutmeg
- 1 tsp ground cinnamon
- 1/2 cup heavy cream
- 1/4 cup Crown Vanilla
- 2 eggs
- Pinch salt
- 1 store-bought graham cracker crust

To serve:
- Whipped cream to taste
- Sprinkle of cinnamon sugar (optional)

Direction

- To a large bowl, add cream cheese, white and brown sugar. Using a hand blender, beat the cream cheese for 2-3 minutes on medium-low speed.
- Mash the boiled potatoes and then spoon them to a bowl with cream cheese. Then add sweet potato.
- Sprinkle with nutmeg, and cinnamon.
- Blend again to incorporate all flavors and add heavy cream, Crown Vanilla, eggs, and salt.
- Mix until smooth and pour cheesecake mixture into a store-bought crust.
- Bake it in preheated oven for 40-45 minutes on 450F.
- Make sure to use middle rack so the crust will not burn.
- After 40-45 minutes turn off the oven and open the oven's door. Allow the cheesecake to cool down inside for 20-30 minutes while the door is opened.
- Then take the cake out and let it cool down for another 30.
- Refrigerate pie overnight
- Top each piece with whipped cream and serve.

Bad & Boozy Banana Pudding

Quick question...
Do you eat your banana pudding with or WITHOUT bananas? Honestly it doesn't matter... Spike it with vanilla crown royal and watch what happens! This is my favorite dessert to make for a group setting, and it never disappoints... like NEVER. Let's get started.

Serving: 8-10

Equipment:
medium bowl, hand mixer, deep glass serving bowl

Prep time: 10 minutes

Total time: 1 hour

Ingredients

- 4-5 large bananas, sliced into bite-sized pieces
- Juice from one large lemon
- 2 cups milk
- 1/2 cup Vanilla Crown Royal Whiskey
- 1 tsp vanilla extract
- 1 (1 oz) packet Jell-O-O, sugar-free vanilla pudding mix
- 1 can (14oz) condensed milk
- 1 - 1.5cup Cool Whip

- 1/2 cup Nilla Wafers, crushed into bite-sized pieces
- 1/2 cup Biscoff cookies, crushed into bite-sized pieces
- 1/2 tsp cinnamon

Direction

- Place sliced bananas into a medium bowl, and drizzle them with lemon juice. Set the bananas aside.
- In a separate bowl, add milk, whiskey, vanilla extract, and pudding mix. Using a hand mixer, blend everything on medium speed for 1-1.5 minutes.
- Next, add condensed milk and Cool Whip. Blend again for one minute.

To assemble:

Follow this layer's order:
1) Bottom layer: 1/2 of Nilla Wafers
2) Top with 1/2 of sliced bananas
3) Pour 1/2 pudding over the bananas and wafers layers.
4) Top with 1/2 of Biscoff cookies
5) Add the rest of the banana slices
6) Cover the banana with the rest of the pudding mix
7) Decorate the top of the pudding with leftover Nilla Wafers.
8) Sprinkle the last layer with cinnamon.

Refrigerate the pudding for at least one hour before serving. Enjoy!

Red Velvet Pound Cake

A super moist and foodgasmic classic… but with a twist! After everyone has DEVOURED the lobster mac, holiday ham, and greens…. Cap off your feast with this moist and flavorful red velvet pound cake. I'll say "you're welcome" in advance

Serving: 8-10

Equipment:
Stand mixer, large bowl, spatula, medium bowl, 13x9 inch pan

Prep time: 2 hours

Cook time: 35 minutes

Ingredients

For the cake:
- 1 stick butter, unsalted, room temperature
- 4 oz cream cheese, room temperature
- 2 cups white sugar
- 3 eggs, room temperature
- 2 cups cake flour
- 2 Tbsp cacao powder
- 240 ml buttermilk (1 cup), room temperature

- 2 tsp baking powder
- 1 Tbsp red food coloring

For the frosting:
- 2 sticks butter, unsalted, room temperature
- 4 oz cream cheese, room temperature
- 1/2 cup sweet condensed milk

Direction

- Using the stand mixer, cream the butter with cream cheese for about 3-4 minutes.
- Add sugar, one tablespoon at a time, and blend until all the sugar is incorporated into the batter.
- Next, add eggs, one at a time.
- Slowly add the cake flour and cacao powder. Blend until combined.
- Remove the mixing bowl from the mixer.
- Gently pour in the buttermilk, baking powder, and red food coloring into it and stir with a spatula until combined. Don't overmix.
- Preheat oven to 350F.
- Pour batter into greased and floured 13x9 inch pan.
- Bake for about 35 minutes, check with a toothpick. If it comes out clean, the cake is made.
- Let it rest at room temperature, then refrigerate it for 30 minutes before frosting with the cream.

For the frosting cream:
- In a medium bowl, combine cream cheese, condensed milk with butter—blend, using a hand blender on low speed until all incorporated.

To assemble:
- Spread the cream over cold cake. Refrigerate for one hour before serving.

Peach Crown Cobbler Rolls

Okay just hear me out. The same soulful and southern classic dessert, but now no fork is required! This is the perfect way to add a little razzle dazzle to your holiday dessert menu!

Serving: 14 rolls

Equipment:
Large skillet

Prep time: 10 minutes

Cook time: 20 minutes

Total time: 30 minutes

Ingredients

- 4 large peaches, washed, peeled
- 1/3 stick butter, unsalted
- 1 tsp rum extract
- 1/4 cup Crown Royal Peach
- 1/2 cup white sugar
- 1/4 cup brown sugar
- 1/2 tsp nutmeg spice
- 1/4 tsp cinnamon

- Pinch allspice
- 14 eggroll sheets/wrappers
- 1/3 cup cooking oil

To serve:
- Vanilla ice-cream

Direction

- Slice peaches into small bite-sized slices.
- Melt butter over low heat and add rum extract and Crown Royal Peach.
- Adjust the heat to high and let the alcohol burn. It will take only one minute or less.
- Then, reduce the heat to low and add white and brown sugar, nutmeg spice, cinnamon, and allspice. Stir and cook for few more minutes. Remove peach mixture from heat and allow it to cool before assembling egg rolls

To assemble:
- Place the eggroll shell wrapper on a cutting board or flat plate. Place about 2 Tbsp of the peach filling in the center. Brush the edges with water, then roll them like a burrito making sure all edges are sealed.
- Repeat with the remaining wrappers.
- Preheat the skillet with oil over medium-high heat and fry the rolls for a few minutes until they are nicely golden.
- Repeat with the remaining rolls.

To serve:
- Serve with vanilla ice cream.

Maple Bacon Glazed Donuts

Bacon makes the world go round!
These Maple Glazed Donuts are covered with cinnamon sugar and smoky, crunchy bacon bits. For a perfect finish, they are glazed with creamy maple glaze. My donuts are super moist and rich in flavor, and very easy to make!

Serving: 5 donuts

Equipment:
Small mason jar or small round cookie cutter, medium skillet, metal tongs, flat plate or cutting board, large pan or skillet, microwavable bowl or cup, basting brash.

Prep time: 15 minutes

Cook time: 10 minutes

Total time: 25 minutes

Ingredients

For the donuts:
- One 12oz can of biscuits
- 1-2 cups cooking oil
- 5 thick bacon slices, chopped
- 1 tsp cinnamon sugar mix

For the glaze:
- 2 Tbsp whipped cream cheese
- 2 tsp brown sugar
- 1/4 cup maple syrup
- Pinch salt
- 1/4 cup heavy cream or full-fat milk

Direction

For the donuts:
- Take two biscuits and stuck one on a top of another.
- Using a small major jar or a round cookie cutter, press in the middle of the donut to make a hole. Repeat with all biscuits, and you will have 5 donuts.
- Preheat the medium deep skillet with cooking oil.
- Carefully place donuts in hot oil, using tongs.
- Fry them for 1-2 minutes on each side until they are golden brown. Don't overcrowd the skillet. Repeat with the rest of the donuts.
- Place donuts on a paper towel to drain any excess oil.
- Prepare the bacon until desired crispiness. You can fry it on a pan or bake it in the oven. It's up to you! I fried my bacon on a large skillet on medium heat for 3 minutes.
- Remove the bacon from the pan and lay it on a paper towel.

For the glaze:
- Add whipped cream cheese, brown sugar, maple syrup, heavy cream, and bacon leftover grease in a microwavable bowl or cup. Whisk the glaze with a fork and microwave it for 30 seconds.

To assemble:
- Lay donuts on a flat plate and brush them with glaze.
- Sprinkle donuts with cinnamon sugar mix, and sprinkle them with bacon pieces.
- Drizzle with more maple syrup if and serve!

Bacon PB&J French Toast

Peanut butter and bacon make everything better, wouldn't you agree?
This sandwich is savory-sweet and smoky with a hint of warm cinnamon and nutmeg! What not to love!

Serving: 2

Equipment:
Large bowl, whisk, large skillet

Prep time: 5 minutes

Cook time: 10 minutes

Total time: 15 minutes

Ingredients

- 3 eggs
- 3/4 cup heavy cream
- 2 tsp vanilla extract
- Pinch nutmeg
- 1/2 tsp cinnamon
- 1/4 cup brown sugar
- 4 slices bacon, thick-cut
- 4 thick cut Challah Bread or Brioche slices

- 1/4 cup peanut butter, unsalted, unsweetened
- 1/4 cup of your favorite jam (strawberry or grape sugar free jelly are the best)
- Powdered sugar for the top

Direction

- Crack the eggs in a bowl and add heavy cream, vanilla extract, nutmeg, cinnamon, and brown sugar.
- Whisk everything together until blended.
- Set this custard aside.
- Preheat a large skillet and add bacon.
- Cook it for about 4 minutes on each side over medium heat.
- Please remove bacon from the skillet and lay it on a paper towel to drain any excess fat. This will make the bacon crispier.
- Spread peanut butter on all four slices of bread, followed by the jam. Top with bacon pieces.
- Place both slices on top of each other.
- Deep the sandwich in a custard, one at the time.
- Add oil to the pan (or use the leftover bacon grease). Fry the sandwich on both sides for 2-3 minutes on each side until lightly brown on medium heat.
- Repeat with the second sandwich.
- •Serve sprinkled with powdered sugar!

Made in United States
Troutdale, OR
03/10/2024